Florida
THEME PARKS
A GUIDE

Alex Miller

Caroline Miller,
Photographer and Illustrator

Foreword by Tony Baxter

Schiffer Publishing Ltd

4880 Lower Valley Road • Atglen, PA 19310

Designed by Danielle D. Farmer
Cover Design by Justin Watkinson
Type set in Aldine 721 BT/Aldine 721 BT

ISBN: 978-0-7643-4333-9
Printed in China

Published by Schiffer Publishing, Ltd.
4880 Lower Valley Road
Atglen, PA 19310
Phone: (610) 593-1777; Fax: (610) 593-2002
E-mail: Info@schifferbooks.com

For the largest selection of fine reference books on this and related subjects, please visit our website at **www.schifferbooks.com.**

You may also write for a free catalog.
This book may be purchased from the publisher.
Please try your bookstore first.

We are always looking for people to write books on new and related subjects. If you have an idea for a book, please contact us at **proposals@schifferbooks.com**

Schiffer Books are available at special discounts for bulk purchases for sales promotions or premiums. Special editions, including personalized covers, corporate imprints, and excerpts can be created in large quantities for special needs. For more information contact the publisher.

In Europe, Schiffer books are distributed by
Bushwood Books
6 Marksbury Ave.
Kew Gardens
Surrey TW9 4JF England
Phone: 44 (0) 20 8392 8585; Fax: 44 (0) 20 8392 9876
E-mail: info@bushwoodbooks.co.uk
Website: www.bushwoodbooks.co.uk

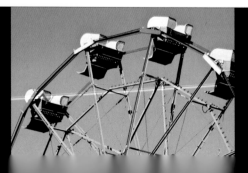

DEDICATION

This book is dedicated to Hanna, my beautiful wife
and lifetime roller coaster companion.

CONTENTS

A GUIDE

* *Italicized names indicate larger resort areas with multiple parks.*

ACKNOWLEDGMENTS

Ten years ago, I was a freshman in high school. That year, one of our school's requirements was that we each take a career aptitude test to help us begin thinking about our future. If you've never taken one of these tests before, I'll walk you through the process. Basically, you sit at a computer for a good hour or so answering questions like:

"Do you enjoy working with your hands?"

"Do you prefer working indoors?"

"Do you like a fast-paced environment?"

Then you slide a bar back and forth stating whether you "Strongly Agree" or "Strongly Disagree." Kind of fun, right? It got me out of freshman English for the day at least.

Do you want to know what the test recommended for me? Zoologist. Pretty cool job, right? I thought so but to be perfectly honest, I never gave it much thought. Ever since I was six—when my parents bought us annual passes to Disneyland—I've known what I wanted to do. I wanted to work for Disney; I wanted to tell great stories and come up with new ways for guests to experience them. For the last twenty years, I've held onto the euphoria I felt as a six-year-old when my family would pack up the van and make the hour-long drive to Anaheim—which was, in my eyes, the greatest city in the world. Those perfect days would always include multiple trips to Splash Mountain, lunch at Village Haus Restaurant in Fantasyland, and—if any of us were feeling particularly brave that day—a terrifying ride through the cosmos on Space Mountain (which was much more about the bragging rights than anything else). It was those childhood trips that defined what I wanted to do with my life, not an aptitude test. Over the years, with the support of many others, I've been able to make my dreams a reality.

I thank my parents, James and Laura Miller, for introducing me to the wonderful world of theme parks at a young age. Thanks to my beautiful wife, Hanna, for indulging my interests and for her constant support. I also offer a special thank you to my good friend and mentor, Dave Pacheco, for his continued guidance; and to Tony Baxter, author of the book's foreword, for his wonderful insight.

I've always found reassurance in the unique way amusement and theme parks unite communities. In the grand scheme of things they sometimes seem trivial—the fact of the matter is, though, they are far from it. As someone who was fortunate enough to grow up around theme parks and then make them a part of my day-to-day life, it always inspires me how loyal patrons defend their nearby park as talks of closing or redevelopment emerge. Attacking someone's local theme park is like attacking their childhood—a sentiment I can definitely relate to. For that, I thank those who have admirably represented their parks and been such an asset to me while writing this book: Kelly Heckinger, Mark Brisson, Lola Parsons, Al Colarusso, Jackie Wallace, Lance Young, Don Rousseau, Richard Sanfilippo, Brooks Jordan, Randi Jong, Dagmar Cardwell, Susan Flower, Brittany Baron, and Rick Sylvain.

Finally, I wouldn't be able to do what I love without the support of two great companies. My sincerest gratitude goes out to the wonderful team at Schiffer Publishing, and to my colleagues at The Walt Disney Company who make each day exciting, challenging, and fun all at once.

But who knows? If I hadn't followed my heart and my wonderful childhood memories, I may have ended up working in a zoo somewhere. And to be fair, zoos and theme parks tend to have quite a bit in common now-a-days. So perhaps my school's aptitude test wasn't wrong, it just couldn't find a name for what my eventual "job" would be.

I like to think so.

FOREWORD

My earliest awareness of Florida occurred in, of all places, a movie theater in the 1950s. It was the Warner Theater on Hollywood Boulevard. The movie was, *This is Cinerama*. The presentation was in the form of a travelogue geared to exploit a mammoth new film format with a wrap-around screen. The high point of the film took viewers to a surreal place in central Florida known as Cypress Gardens. To a five-year-old, bathed in images of a tropical paradise with exotic birds and antebellum maidens along the banks of a botanical wonderland, that footage became iconic for what I would forever expect Florida to be.

The *Cinerama* format was invented by Fred Waller, who also held the patent for water skis. By "coincidence," a good part of the Cypress Gardens sequence took viewers into the water to demonstrate how much fun you could have speeding across Florida's lakes on those sporty toys. The overall impression was of a paradise found, where time stood still and play was the order of the day. To an impressionable little kid, for whom the world of theme parks would not exist for several years, Cypress Gardens would serve as a golden dream for years to come.

A decade later, my best friend and his family actually got the chance to travel from California to Florida. The slides they took on that vacation ignited my dreams of Florida. Here was a world of pink flamingos, seashell-strewn beaches, clear mermaid pools, alligator-filled swamps, and tropical jungles. That recharged passion would have to remain on hold until the spring of 1971, when The Walt Disney Company took up residency in central Florida.

At that time, I was a design assistant to legendary Imagineer, Claude Coats, in Glendale, California. I soon found myself on a plane, leaving the land of earthquakes for Florida, which turned out to have its own surprises of nature. This was my first time living outside California, and when I stepped off onto the primitive McCoy Airfield in Orlando, I wasn't prepared for the blast of high humidity or the clockwork afternoon rain shower. The natural beauty of Florida comes with a price ... lush environments require lots of water, and daily!

The Walt Disney World construction site was initially very isolated from urban Orlando. Once you entered the 27,000 acres of Disney property, the only "comforts" available were located in the administration center about five miles from the Magic Kingdom worksite. I was partnering with Dave Burkhart on both of Claude Coats's opening day attractions: 20,000 Leagues Under the Sea, and Snow White's Adventures. Snow White was indoors, but "Leagues" was mostly out in the full sun. Air conditioning would not be installed anywhere for months, and I gained respect for what the combination of high temperature and humidity can do to the human body. On Saturdays I would often see my ambitious sightseeing plans fade after stepping out of my apartment into a blast of hot summer heat. It felt so right to abort the plans and spend the rest of the day lounging in the pool.

As a bona fide "geek" for anything vaguely "theme park," I did manage to see many of the sights in Florida that were soon to vanish as a direct result of the dreams we were laboring to bring to life. I realized my childhood "Cinerama" fantasy by visiting Dick Pope's Cypress Gardens, even opting for a season pass. Then there was the Weeki Wachee, Spring of Live Mermaids, noted as the location for the most outrageous movie premiere ever. In 1964, the world premiere of *The Incredible Mr. Limpet* unspooled underwater at Weeki Wachee. "Live" mermaids distracted the audience from the on screen antics of star Don Knotts!

North of Orlando, crystal clear waters that flowed through attractions around Ocala, Rainbow Springs, and Silver Springs. Silver Springs was the filming site for the legendary 3D epic *The Creature from the Black Lagoon*. This was also the neighborhood where one could find "Six Gun Territory," a Knott's Berry Farm want-to-be that never quite managed to transport visitors to the arid Wild West. Tropic landscapes and high humidity is not quite where you expect to meet up with John Wayne!

Closer to Orlando (the still active), "Gatorland" sated appetites for dangerous thrills and creepy curiosity, while an hour drive to the western shores would get me to Tampa, the historic home of Busch Gardens (when it was only a garden). Just beyond, in nearby Clearwater, was the memorable Kapok Tree Restaurant. This was an amazing themed dining experience, and even today I wish it were possible to return.

These were all simple roadside attractions, iconic symbols of the myth that may have begun with the search for Florida's legendary fountain of youth. When I arrived in Orlando nobody could really foresee what dramatic cultural forces were at work and how they would transform the Florida landscape over the decades closing out the twentieth century.

For me, this all began to sink in during late August of 1971. I had found my own special Florida paradise at the end of a dirt road on Disney property. Soon, this road would be feeding campers into the Fort Wilderness Campground at the Disney World Resort, but for a few more golden Sundays of summer, it would be my gateway to the dream-like Florida of my childhood. I would drive my car as far as I dared before the soft, sandy road became treacherous, and then hike onward to the beautifully secluded shores of Bay Lake. Not a human sound could be heard, nor was there any evidence of people lapping up the clear water and sunshine on its pristine beach. In the quiet of the moment the reality hit me that very soon this would all end. The lake, which had been mine alone on these magical weekends, would soon belong to the world.

Disney set the entertainment bar so high in Florida that competition would scramble for years to learn how to react to it. Many roadside attractions would vanish from the scene; others would have to adapt to live on. Physical transformation would ultimately be ignited by an economy that basked in the glow of some of the greatest themed destinations in the world. These parks and resorts have reached out in highly creative ways to meet the gauntlet laid down by Walt Disney World over forty years ago.

This book gives great insight into the Florida Theme Parks as they exist today, but if you get a hankering to return back to the roadside wonders of Florida's yesteryears, just head on down Highway 27 to Lake Wales to visit the Bok Singing Tower, then stop by Chalet Suzanne for a real taste of authentic Florida cuisine in a historic folk architecture setting. A themed visit to Florida is not complete without a delicious broiled grapefruit and "Moon Soup" from Chalet Suzanne. Yes, this is the only soup ever served on the moon!

—Tony Baxter
Senior Vice President,
Walt Disney Imagineering

INTRODUCTION

"The Sunshine State," that's what they call it … and for good reason. Florida's tropical climate has made it a "destination state" for Americans seeking to escape the colder northern weather for ages. Florida also boasts the longest coastline of any of the lower forty-eight states, which is especially impressive when you consider that no point in the state of Florida is ever more than two hours from the nearest beach. But beaches and sunshine aren't the only things guests come looking for. In less than fifty years, Florida's blossoming travel industry has earned recognition as the theme park resort center of the world. How that came to be is a fairly interesting story.

While amusement and themed attraction parks have existed in some sense for hundreds of years, the modern American theme park industry we know today began in California, where a legacy of century-old seaside amusements fused with new ideas of storytelling and family entertainment. Florida, however, perfected that industry—transforming roughly 100 square miles of undeveloped swampland into world-leading family-vacation destinations.

If you visited the state in the early 1960s, you would have been greeted by a much different Florida—a Florida whose primary industries were citrus and cattle ranching. That Florida of yesteryear was not a one-stop shop; but a menagerie of roadside oddities ranging from botanical gardens and alligator farms to river excursions, observation towers, and almost anything else imaginable. Most of these attractions were short-lived but, fortunately, Florida has never lacked imagination. And as soon as one of these roadside attractions closed, a new idea was always ready to take its place, keeping Florida's highways an ever-changing amalgam of one-of-a-kind curiosities. However, on November 15th, 1965, that world was changed forever.

On that day, accompanied by his business partner and older brother, Roy, as well as Florida governor W. Haydon Burns, entertainment pioneer Walt Disney, announced the development of a new Disney attraction slated for central Florida. Details

at the press event were modest but by the end, Governor Burns felt comfortable declaring the day "The most important day in the progress of the future development of this state," stating that he knew "of no single thing in history that could have made the impact that the establishment of a Disney facility here will make."

Disney's purchase of central Florida land was unprecedented. When building Disneyland® Park in Anaheim, California, the company sought 160 acres. At the time, that expanse of land even seemed excessive to those who couldn't understand Walt Disney's vision. What Walt had planned for Florida, however, was much, much greater. Leading up to the November press conference, Disney had managed to acquire over 27,000 acres of central Florida land—more than 150 times the original land purchase in Anaheim. The rationale for that was simple—Walt Disney was looking to build a city.

EPCOT, an Experimental Prototype Community of Tomorrow (sometimes also referred to as Experimental Prototype City of Tomorrow), was Walt's last great dream. Envisioned as a utopia with 20,000 residents, the planned city would be a haven for community and innovation. Feeling that the cities of the day were polluted and chaotic, Walt's intricate plan was comprised of revolutionary ideas in transportation, industry, and day-to-day living. Pioneering corporations could take up residence in the city, which would be used to showcase unending progress in all fields. Walt Disney's hope was that EPCOT would inspire visitors to return home and seek ways to improve their own cities. Per the request of Disney's board of directors, who wanted assurance that people would come to see this city of tomorrow, the Florida site would also include a Magic Kingdom® theme park inspired by Disneyland®. Visitors could then spend their time touring the city and its innovative industrial park, and finally move on to Magic Kingdom® Park at the end.

Sadly, Walt Disney passed away before his dream could be realized, but spent some of his last days happily planning the city on his hospital bed ceiling. With the captain no longer steering the ship, Walt's older brother and lifetime business partner, Roy Disney, postponed his retirement to oversee his brother's final project through to the finish. While he couldn't convince the board to green light EPCOT, he did oversee the completion of Magic Kingdom® Park, and dedicated Walt Disney World to the life and philosophy of his younger brother. Roy Disney passed away just two months later.

As time would soon tell, Governor Burns's prophecy could not have been more true. In October 1971, The Walt Disney Company cut the ribbon on what would become the most visited theme park in the entire world, Magic Kingdom® Park. Despite the fact that it was a far cry from the original concept Walt dreamt up for Florida, guests would flock to the former swampland. Like-minded entertainment companies followed shortly after, transforming tourism into the state's leading industry.

Disney's surplus of land in Florida allowed for constant expansion—a luxury that had never been readily available in California. After a few short years, Disney began revisiting the EPCOT idea—only this time, as a theme park, not a city. In the early '80s, nearly a quarter century after Walt Disney drafted some of the earliest concepts of the project, Disney unveiled EPCOT Center, a park loosely inspired by Walt's original vision. It was the first theme park to exceed $1,000,000,000 in cost. Many more parks, attractions, and tourism venues would follow from some of the world's top entertainment companies as Florida quickly assumed its new identity as the world's theme park resort leader.

With the agility that Florida first used to refresh its roadside attractions, the state has embraced its new role as leader in family entertainment. The University of Central Florida now even offers a Bachelors Degree in Hospitality Management with a specialized track for Theme Park and Attraction Management. Several altruistic organizations, like Give Kids The World Village, make their home in central Florida—allowing families to enjoy the wonderful venues while their children receive treatment. And every year, millions upon millions of families make their way to the Sunshine State, eager to enjoy the theme parks that have come to be known so well throughout the globe.

With so many diverse experiences, this book is meant to be used as a guide to that magic. In each chapter, you'll find an overview of each park with a breakdown of its key attractions. Hopefully you'll take away a feel for the unique magic that exists in each one. I know I did.

Busch Gardens Tampa Bay

TAMPA BAY, FLORIDA

Over the years, Busch Gardens' tropical landscape and exotic animals have transformed the venue into a full-fledged African theme park—complete with bazaar-style shops.

A view of the Serengeti Plain from the park's Skyride.

OPERATED BY SEAWORLD PARKS AND ENTERTAINMENT, visitors may find it odd that this famed African-themed park bears the name of the well-known American brewery, Anheuser-Busch. When it opened in 1959, however, it was an admission-free hospitality facility for the now defunct beer manufacturing plant. Over the years, the modest tropical garden and animal shows expanded to include the rides and animal habitats that would eventually make the park famous. Adventure Island, an accompanying water park, also operates just across the street.

Busch Gardens Tampa Bay is divided up into ten lands—each representing different African countries, cities, or uniquely African experiences. In addition, this forward-thinking theme park also offers what was the first free-roaming animal habitat of its kind, the Serengeti Plain. Unlike many zoos in 1965, which were much more like animal prisons than habitats, Busch Gardens Tampa pioneered a new concept of animal habitation; a wide open area where many different, non-aggressive species could roam freely together. Guests can view this habitat from a train that circumnavigates the park, or the Skyride, a gondola that passes over the Serengeti. The park's newest land, Cheetah Hunt, features an identically named roller coaster that offers fantastic—and thrilling—views of the Plain while cruising high above it at sixty mph.

Busch Garden's nation-inspired lands, Morocco, Egypt, and Congo, feature some of the park's biggest thrills. Gwazi, one of Florida's very few wooden roller coasters, has more "fly-bys" than any other dueling roller coaster in the world. With two coaster tracks, Lion and Tiger, the coaster trains will pass by each other six times on each ride. Montu and Kumba,

Like the shikra, an African hawk known for its vertical dive, the SheiKra roller coaster provides an equally steep drop. Falling 200 feet, guests will reach the top speed of 70 mph in a matter of seconds.

Wooden roller coasters are especially rare in Florida due to the high upkeep costs associated with operating in a tropical climate. Gwazi, however, is actually two rides in one—a fact many wooden coaster fans will appreciate.

Kumba—meaning "roar" in the African language of Kongo—will have riders doing just that through the roller coaster's seven inversions.

two of the world's most popular coasters, will test any thrill-seeker up to the challenge of taming them.

While the park's city-named lands may showcase some exciting rides—like SheiKra, North America's first dive coaster famous for its 90° 200-foot drop—Stanleyville, Timbuktu, and Nairobi offer many attractions that don't necessarily require a daredevil attitude to enjoy. Stanleyville, named after the former Congo River city, appropriately features two popular water attractions: the Stanley Falls Flume and the Tanganyika Tidal Wave. Nairobi offers several safari tours, including the popular Rhino Rally, an off-road excursion through the wild African veldt. Timbuktu, inspired by the bazaar-rich African city, features a variety of smaller attractions as well as two coasters, the Scorpion and SandSerpent.

Another water ride, the Congo River Rapids, offers a wet and wild trip through the jungle, past caves and waterfalls.

Though perhaps not as hot as some real African cities, Tampa Bay can reach impressive highs, making a trip down a waterfall a welcome thought by mid-afternoon.

The park's final themed lands, Sesame Street Safari of Fun, Jungala, and Bird Gardens, are most popular with younger explorers. Many Sesame Street stars have their own attraction at the safari; hop on Elmo's Safari Go-Round or splash around at Bert and Ernie's Watering Hole. Catch a flight at Air Grover, or meet all your favorite friends at Big Bird's 123–Smile with Me. For those looking for a more animal-friendly exhibition, Jungala offers some great animal encounters and even a zip line for young adventurers. Bird Gardens, the park's original hospitality zone, still features animal shows, gardens, and a free-flight aviary.

While it may have started out as a brewery, Busch Gardens Tampa Bay has grown into much more. Thrilling rides and exotic animals make it one superb safari.

Elmo's Treehouse Trek gives a (Big-) Birds-eye view of the entire Sesame Street Safari of Fun.

Chart a course over rope bridges and nets in Jungala—home to some unique wildlife.

While it has evolved considerably over more than half a century, Busch Gardens still maintains its namesake botanical attractions.

A Busch Gardens resident surveys his surroundings at the Edge of Africa. With everything the park has to offer, guests of all sizes will be able to "find" a good time.

2
Fun Spot America

ORLANDO, FLORIDA

The original entrance to Fun Spot—a place with many exciting developments in store!

Constantly pushing the boundaries, Fun Spot America is known for its multi-level go-cart tracks. Several patented features have kept them speeding ahead of the competition.

DESPITE BEING LOCATED IN THE HEART OF ORLANDO, most "out-of-staters" will never have heard of Fun Spot America. And while the rest of the world stampedes to visit central Florida's larger theme parks, Orlandians have somehow managed to keep this exhilarating little park a secret for well over a decade. Given the fact that they don't have to compete with the crowds of other major parks in the area, it's likely a secret guests will try to keep to themselves for as long as possible!

Fun Spot America opened in 1998. Originally a family entertainment center (as opposed to a full-fledged amusement park), the park quickly developed a reputation for its thrilling go-carts. It currently offers four exciting tracks that guests won't be able to find anywhere else—literally. Go-cart industry veteran and park president, John Arie Sr., has developed and patented several one-of-a-kind thrills that make Fun Spot's go-carts a little more "extreme" than the competition.

Unlike the go-carts, guests are encouraged to bump each other on this classic ride.

The Paratrooper waits patiently for another round of fun-seekers.

The park attractions extend much further than go-carts though. Classic amusements like a Ferris wheel, carousel, and bumper cars are popular with the whole family. A kiddie train, kiddie swings, spinning tea cups, and Super Trucks then make up the park's "preschool" ride section. Those who haven't gotten their adrenaline-fill from the go-carts will also enjoy two classic thrills—Paratrooper and a Scrambler. Bumper boats, Fun Slide, a Frog Hopper free-fall attraction, and a 10,000 square foot arcade round out the par , including finger puppets, table runners, sunflower bowls, rings, and purses. k attractions. With several event rooms, Fun Spot is popular not only as a birthday party venue but also offers several team building events and activities that incorporate the rides. The best for this park, however, is still yet to come.

Even though a section of the park is called Kid Spot, parents can enjoy riding with their little ones on most of the park's "preschool" rides.

Of course, we all have to start somewhere! The Cadet Track is perfect for young racers to hone their hairpin turns.

At 10,000 square feet, Fun Spot's two-story arcade has something for every gamer—from classic to cutting edge.

The park's Scrambler will shortly be joined by more thrills as Fun Spot continues to grow.

Eager drivers prepare for a race on one of the park's signature tracks.

Soon, Fun Spot's rotating rides will be joined by slippery slides as the park adds on water park attractions.

Recently, Fun Spot announced a multi-year expansion project which—when complete— will more than triple the park's size. Included in the plans are two exciting roller coasters and more than a handful of additional thrill rides. Skycoaster, a free-fall attraction that headlines Fun Spot's other amusement park in Kissimmee, Florida, will be replicated at this Orlando park. Plans for water slides, a lazy river, and wave pool are also included in the expansion, transforming what was once a family entertainment center into an all-day amusement and water park experience. Naturally, an expansion project of this size merited a re-christening. Originally known as Fun Spot Action Park, it adopted the name Fun Spot America as part of the transformation.

It's often surprising when a small regional amusement park begins to compete with its much larger neighbors. Fun Spot Action Park, however, has flourished in Orlando. If its past successes are any indication of what's to come, Orlandians may have to face the fact that their "secret" park will soon be a destination amusement park for "out-of-staters" as well. In the words of Fun Spot president, John Arie, "Life is Great!"; surely that's the case at Fun Spot America.

Fun Spot's bright future will keep their big wheel turning for years of future enjoyment.

While still very young, the park has quickly expanded to become an all-day family amusement park.

3

Fun Spot USA

KISSIMMEE, FLORIDA

Like its sister-park in Orlando, Fun Spot USA's main entrance welcomes guests through a large arcade before they reach the rides.

With plenty of games and the park's largest snack bar, the arcade is a "fun spot" to relax and refuel.

A SISTER-PARK TO THE ORIGINAL FUN SPOT PARK IN ORLANDO, Fun Spot USA has quickly grown into a standout family amusement park on its own. Opened in 2007, the park offers some exciting thrills wrapped up nicely into an experience the whole family will enjoy. Guests unfamiliar with the Kissimmee area should note that Fun Spot USA is actually so close to the nearby Old Town amusement park, the two actually share some parking lots.

After Fun Spot's Orlando park opened in 1998, Fun Spot President, John Arie Sr., began looking for a larger site for his next family entertainment venture. The town of Kissimmee, just fifteen miles south, proved to be the answer. The site also had a unique draw: it was already home to the world's tallest "SkyCoaster."

The 300–foot Kissimmee icon is still the park's headline attraction. Guests visiting the area will notice the prominent towers day or night, beckoning thrill seekers to one of Florida's most extreme amusement attractions. Perched scenically over a small lake, guests brave enough to take on the SkyCoaster will slowly ascend to 300 feet above the city. Because central Florida is relatively flat, riders will literally be able to see for miles once they reach the top—that is, if they're able to open their eyes! Once they pull the

While the park does offer a "Road Course" and "Slick Track," their other go-cart tracks are far from flat. The Vortex, seen here, features a challenging 2° banked bowl that will keep competitors coming back again and again.

Drivers navigate an upward helix on one of Fun Spot's multi-level go-cart tracks.

rip cord, they'll find themselves hurtling back to earth before they swoop up and over the rest of the park again, reaching speeds of 85 mph.

As with the original Orlando venue, it wouldn't be a Fun Spot park without go-carts. Fun Spot USA also features some exciting multi-level tracks with patented thrills that guests won't find anywhere else. In addition, the spinning Power Trip Coaster offers plenty of twists, turns, and drops for those who prefer not to "drive the ride." Guests who want a thrill without the dizziness of the coaster will likely enjoy the park's Hot Seat attraction most of all.

Opened in 1997, the SkyCoaster delighted patrons for ten years before Fun Spot USA began operation in Kissimmee. Today, the park offers attractions that can be enjoyed by more than just thrill-seekers.

With several seconds of complete freefall, guests plummet 300 feet on the SkyCoaster. Those brave enough to ride it twice might want try it once during the day and once at night to enjoy two unique views of central Florida.

The spinning Power Trip Coaster prepares for some dizzying drops ahead.

At the far end of the park, guests will discover quite a few all-family attractions they can enjoy together.

The aptly named Kid Spot section of the park has rides for younger guests.

Fun Spot USA is laid out in an oval around the park's miniature lake. On the bank, fun-seekers will find a wide variety of nearly twenty carnival-style rides. Screamin Eagles, Flying Bobs, and Paratrooper will delight both young and old alike while rides like Convoy, Cyber Jets, and Baron Planes are meant exclusively for smaller guests. Those with an eye for classics will also enjoy the Tilt-A-Whirl, swings, and bumper cars, three of history's most iconic "old time" amusement attractions. Outside the rides, guests can enjoy a large arcade and outdoor carnival games.

Like its sister-park in Orlando, Fun Spot USA has thrived in the theme park Mecca of Central Florida. With the classic flair of a good old-fashioned amusement park, Fun Spot USA also offers excitement and challenges for the thrill seeker. Already a favorite among locals, this young park has a bright future ahead of it.

Though it doesn't hurt, Fun Spot visitors don't need to win a prize to take home a good time!

Kiddie Coaster begins its short climb.

Located in an area known for its natural land reserves, this quaint little park has offered another family-fun option to visitors for decades.

4

King Richard's Family Fun Park

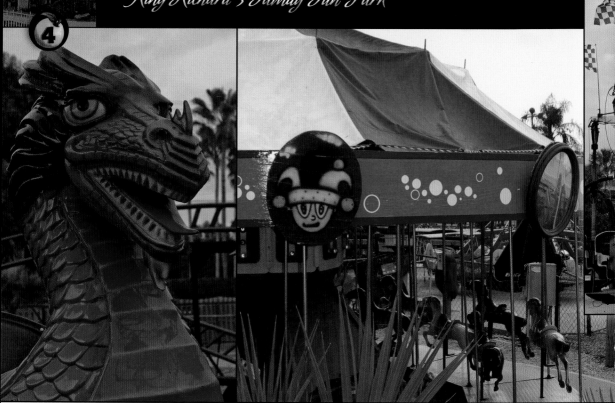

No castle theme park would be complete without a dragon—a dragon roller coaster that is.

King Richard's offers a few rides exclusively for their smallest guests.

WHILE THE WORD "TOURISM" IS ALMOST SYNONYMOUS WITH SOUTH Florida, the area is not known for amusement or theme parks. With its beautiful white-sand beaches, limitless golf courses, and the popular Key West, Southern Florida is a haven for sun-loving vacationers. Everglades National Park, Ten Thousand Islands, and a variety of wildlife sanctuaries also make the region a place of wonderful, natural beauty. However, those looking for another nearby family activity should make a procession to King Richard's Family Fun Park.

The self-proclaimed "#1 stop for fun in Naples, Florida" has been entertaining local families since it first opened in 1990. While the park does offer batting cages, go-cart tracks, and an impressive castle themed arcade—all the mainstay attractions of a typical family fun center—it's a little more than that. King Richard's has several family thrill rides, including Knights of the Round Table and Tornado—two exciting spin attractions—and Dungeon Drop, a miniature free fall tower. Dragon Wagon, the park's lone roller coaster is a popular ride the whole family can enjoy together. For the younger and perhaps less thrill-inclined, there are several age-appropriate rides as well. A miniature merry-go-round and Ferris wheel along with a few additional kiddie attractions are also on-hand for enjoyment.

Since guests control their spinning on the Tornado, they may want to choose their riding partners carefully!

Poised and ready for action, go-carts stand ready to take guests on a high speed tour of the park. Smaller riders can ride alongside an adult, or take the wheel themselves on the park's smaller tracks.

From there, the park expands out to a miniature golf course and several children's play areas. Indoor attractions like laser tag and rock climbing can be enjoyed rain or shine. Like many smaller amusement parks and family fun centers, King Richard's is a popular venue for children's birthday parties. However, kids aren't the only ones who can enjoy parties here; the park also offers a popular "NFL Ticket" package during football season at a restaurant where members can enjoy each Sunday game on 15 HD TV's, with access to the full service kitchen and bar.

Like many castles, King Richard's also has a moat. But unlike its medieval counterparts, which may have kept their moats stocked with sea serpents, this park has something a little more Floridian guarding the castle: alligators. For over a century, Sunshine State tourists have been fascinated by this wetland reptile. While Florida and other neighboring states have become accustomed to sharing land with this apex predator, the American alligator inhabits only the southeast region of the country. For those from out of state or out of the country, coming in contact with an alligator has always been viewed as a true Florida novelty. At King Richard's Alligator Encounter, guests can also purchase alligator food to feed these hungry castle guardians.

With all that there is to do in South Florida, King Richard's is often overlooked by tourists visiting the area. However, for families passing through Naples on their way to the beach or a wildlife preserve, the park makes for a wonderful afternoon. Enjoyed by locals for almost a quarter century now, King Richard's will offer a regal family experience for years to come.

Though it doesn't quite fit in with the park's castle motif, you can bet that the delighted children riding the Ferris wheel don't mind.

Come meet Florida's official state reptile at the Gator Encounter. The American alligator has long been an animal of interest for visitors to the Sunshine State.

A hungry alligator waits for a hand out.

Winter Haven residents received a wonderful treat when LEGOLAND® Florida opened its gates just two years after the final closure of Cypress Gardens.

5

LEGOLAND

Florida

LEGOLAND® Florida has gone to great lengths to preserve the heritage of Cypress Gardens. Here, a rather "blocky" Southern Belle enjoys the botanical gardens restored to their former glory.

INSPIRED BY THE INGENUITY AND IMAGINATION OF EVERYONE'S favorite building brick, this park is a paradise for children—as well as parents—who grew up playing with LEGO® toys. One of Florida's newest theme parks, LEGOLAND® Florida opened on October 15th, 2011. However, despite the park's newness, it is actually located in one of the most historic tourist locations in all of Florida.

Up until 2009, this Winter Haven site was home to Cypress Gardens, a pioneering botanical-garden-turned-theme-park that operated for over seventy years. Facing the prospect of permanent closure for quite some time, this iconic park finally hung up its shears for the last time in 2009 ... or so they thought. Just a few months later, Merlin Entertainments—operators of the popular LEGOLAND® parks—purchased the now defunct Cypress Gardens and LEGO® bricks were able to do what they've done for decades—rebuild.

Cypress Gardens was known for three things: beautiful gardens, Southern Belles, and amazing water ski shows. In a 30–acre area of the park, LEGOLAND® was able to preserve the park's heritage—and in LEGOLAND's Pirates' Cove, has honored Cypress Gardens' notoriety as the water-ski capital of the world, with a LEGO® twist!

An imaginative tribute to one of water-skiing's most historic venues, LEGOLAND® Florida offers a swashbuckling show at Pirates' Cove.

For those looking to take home more than pictures, The Big Shop offers a great selection of LEGO® sets and souvenirs.

From beginning to end, discover what goes into the making of a LEGO® brick.

Outside the historic botanical garden and Pirates' Cove, the park offers nine additional themed lands. The Beginning, Fun Town, and Miniland USA, are perhaps the three most iconic LEGO® experiences. Stop by The Big Shop and choose from countless LEGO® sets—the perfect souvenir for a LEGO® themed park. Take a factory tour and watch as LEGO® bricks are created right before your eyes. Make your way through the heart of LEGOLAND® at Miniland USA and see some of America's most famous landmarks recreated in miniature with millions of LEGO® bricks. Florida natives will recognize the Kennedy Space Center and Daytona International Speedway® amongst other landmarks from California, New York, Washington D.C., and Las Vegas.

LOST KINGDOM
ADVENTURE

With blasters in hand,
riders navigate Lost
Kingdom Adventure
in search of targets
and treasure. Those
with the sharpest eye
and quickest finger will
emerge victorious.

NASA
UNITED STATES
USA

Countdown to ignition—and liftoff!
Miniland USA is a re-creation of iconic
U.S. cities and locations with several
sections dedicated to the theme park's
home state of Florida.

Originally known as the Triple Hurricane when opened by Cypress Gardens, this wooden roller coaster recently received a prehistoric makeover. Today, guests will encounter a dino-sized thrill that's fun for the whole family.

Pick up your lance and take on other knights at the Royal Joust.

Recreating in miniature is one thing. But LEGOLAND® also takes guests into the worlds created by each of its sets at Land of Adventure, LEGO® Kingdoms, and DUPLO® Village. Head back in time to ride the Coastersaurus, or take aim at the supernatural on the off-road laser attraction, Lost Kingdom Adventure. Saddle up for the Royal Joust or step into a castle and tame The Dragon at the park's medieval themed LEGO® Kingdom. The smallest guests, who haven't yet started playing with LEGO® sets, will enjoy DUPLO® village, a land named after LEGO's larger brick for young children.

Captain a vessel through the LEGO® City waterways at Boating School.

Perhaps the most exciting feature LEGO® sets can offer, however, is the ability to turn imagination into reality. LEGOLAND® Florida's last three lands, LEGO® City, LEGO® TECHNIC™, and Imagination Zone reflect that excitement. Learn to drive, fly, or sail at various attractions in LEGO® City. Experience the physics of construction and even several "self-powered" rides at LEGO® TECHNIC™ and Imagination Zone. Build and test a LEGO® dragster and compete with friends on several timed tracks.

Even with over 50 million LEGO®
bricks used throughout the park, it's
the attention to detail that makes
LEGOLAND® Florida so special.

LEGO® has fulfilled the desire to create for decades. In tandem, LEGOLAND® Florida and its neighbor, LEGOLAND® Water Park, have rebuilt a Florida tourism legacy.

Filled with LEGO® activities, Imagination Zone encourages guests to create their own fun.

With the addition of Miracle Strip to Pier Park, this outdoor mall now offers rides alongside its vast selection of shops and restaurants.

Miracle Strip at Pier Park

PANAMA CITY BEACH, FLORIDA

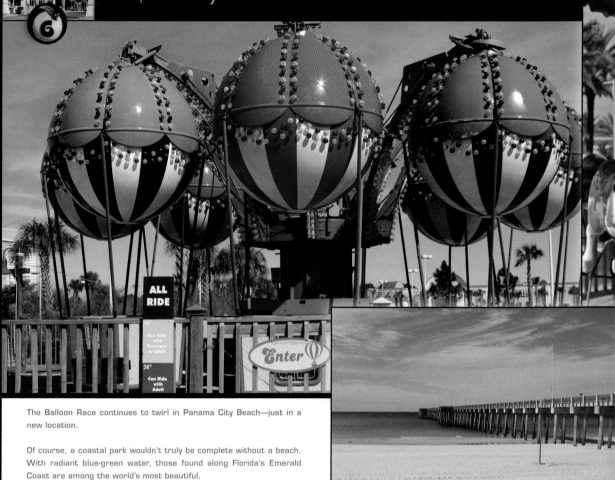

The Balloon Race continues to twirl in Panama City Beach—just in a new location.

Of course, a coastal park wouldn't truly be complete without a beach. With radiant blue-green water, those found along Florida's Emerald Coast are among the world's most beautiful.

SECOND ONLY TO ALASKA IN THE U.S., Florida has a longer coastline than any other state in the lower forty-eight at well over 1,000 miles. Despite that impressive feat, however, Florida has only enjoyed a handful of seaside parks over the last century—in part due to the constant threat of tropical storms. Unlike California and New York, which still operate several famous coastal amusement parks dating back to the 1920s Golden Age of Amusement Parks, Miracle Strip Amusement Park was Florida's last full-fledged oceanside amusement park. When it closed in 2004, along with its headline attraction, the Starliner wooden roller coaster, it looked as though Florida's seaside park industry had finally dried up—save for a few amusement centers scattered along the coast.

Panama City Beach has evolved quite a bit since the original Miracle Strip Amusement Park opened in 1963. Formerly a family vacation hot spot, the town grew into a popular "spring break" destination over the years, drawing fewer families. Sometimes a change in location, however, is all it takes to revive a beloved landmark. In 2009, a couple named Teddy and Jenny Meeks decided to give Miracle Strip another chance. They purchased a few of the rides from the original location, and began relocating them a few miles down the road to an outdoor shopping center called Pier Park. The attractions flourished, and Miracle Strip got a second lease on life.

As magnificent as it was in its heyday, this 1964 Allan Herschel Carousel was the first ride saved following the closure of the original Miracle Strip Amusement Park. Guests touring the new park today will likely pick up on the strong sense of Americana that is alive and well in this small seaside treasure.

The entrance sign to the park's Red Baron ride—complete with the date and manufacturer for amusement park history enthusiasts.

The Sea Dragon prepares for a wavy voyage.

As one might expect, Miracle Strip at Pier Park features several classic amusement rides. The park's carousel, Red Baron, and Tilt-A-Whirl were all among attractions from the former park—refurbished back to pristine condition. Where the new park couldn't get hold of the original attractions, they sought out rides that were the same make and model to keep the small park historically accurate. Seaside park fans may recognize that Miracle Strip's Ferris wheel, The Big Eli, actually operated at California's Santa Monica Pier before arriving in Florida. Mindful of preserving amusement park nostalgia, each attraction features a placard that tells the date each ride was built. Young guests may enjoy knowing that their grandparents rode those exact attractions decades earlier. With a sock hop jumping pillow, butterfly pavilion, and several other rides and attractions, Miracle Strip at Pier Park is sure to make any child's trip to the outdoor mall a little more exciting. To top it off, Miracle Strip managed to secure the original Starliner roller coaster for future generations to enjoy.

Butte
PAVI

REOPEN
MARCH 1ST

Enter

Nature enthusiasts will enjoy the Butterfly Pavilion, which features a variety of native butterflies.

Though it crossed the country to do so, Miracle Strip's Ferris wheel now offers beautiful views out into the Gulf of Mexico. Years earlier, riders of this attraction would have been treated to an equally breathtaking Pacific Ocean panorama.

Outside Miracle Strip, guests have just a short walk to the beautiful white-sand beaches. Passing by several beach-friendly stores and restaurants along the way, visitors can literally spend the whole day at Pier Park while enjoying sun, rides, and an age-old seaside park experience. With such dedication to preserving its history, Miracle Strip at Pier Park may yet prove to be Florida's seaside park savior.

When was the last time you had fun like this? With shops and rides from a bygone era, certainly it's been a while!

WHEN WAS

THE LAST TIME

YOU HAD FUN

LIKE THIS

Bumper Cars
Lazer Tag
Straight Ahead at the
Front of Old Town

7

Old Town

KISSIMMEE, FLORIDA

7

Nostalgic guests will enjoy turning back the clock in this old fashioned amusement park.

An excited patron zip-lines past the Ferris wheel at the front end of Old Town theme park.

FLORIDA IS RENOWNED FOR ITS TROPICAL WEATHER; as such, it's developed a reputation as the ideal retirement state. Naturally, a tourist area inspired by mid-century America is a perfect fit in the theme park rich region of central Florida. Literally a living history of rides, shops, and eateries, Old Town has been offering a trip to yesteryear for all its guests since it opened in 1986.

The park is laid out in a unique fashion. Essentially, it's a pedestrian friendly street that spans several blocks. Split between the far north and south ends of the street, Old Town offers roughly twenty rides and attractions while an amalgam of unique stores and restaurants fill the walk in between.

No old-fashioned amusement park would be complete without the most iconic attraction of all—a carousel.

Rocketing through the sky, riders will reach an altitude of several hundred feet before plummeting back to earth on the Slingshot. Those brave enough to ride will get the chance to relive the experience afterward thanks to an on-ride camera that captures the entire episode.

The Rock Climbing Wall is part of Old Town's AMPVenture Experience—a state of the art, multi-faceted challenge course.

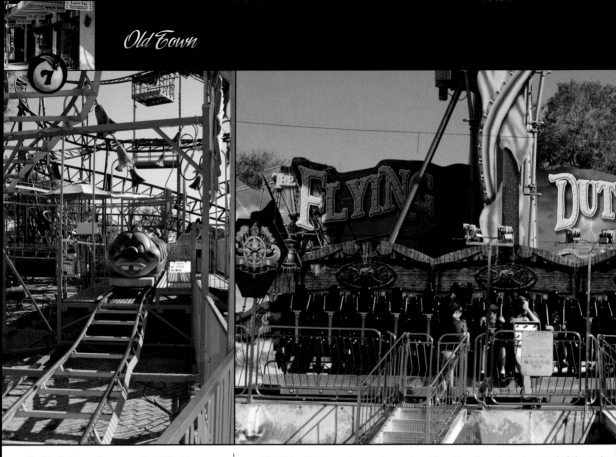

The Wacky Worm (foreground) and Windstorm coaster (background) cover a fair amount of ground in the back half of the park.

The Flying Dutchman is one of several exciting attractions at the front end of the park.

The park's front end mixes some classic attractions—like the Century Ferris Wheel and Bumper Cars—with a few modern thrills. The Drop Zone Super Shot and nearby Slingshot will provide a heart-pounding ride through the sky with fantastic views of Old Town below. AMPVenture Experience, a four-story obstacle course offers a rope challenge, rock wall, and zip line, while go-carts, laser tag, and a few other rides round out the remaining front end attractions.

At the back end, just a few blocks away, guests will encounter an even greater variety of rides. The Windstorm Roller Coaster is an attraction thrill-seekers won't want to miss. For thrill-seekers in training, the Wacky Worm coaster might be more their speed. Visitors will find a wide variety of children's rides at the back end and true to its roots, the park wouldn't be complete without a Tilt-A-Whirl or a selection of midway games.

Browsing through the eclectic Old Town shops can be an experience in itself.

Guests will encounter all sorts of unique items as they meander through the Old Town stores.

Delectable sweets and sugary gumballs line the shelves at an Old Town candy shop. In it, customers will find everything they need to satisfy their sweet tooth.

While some may come for the rides, Old Town has a lot more to offer in between. With over fifty shops, restaurants, and novelties, guests have quite a few options to choose from. Create your own jewelry and accessories, or sample the goods at an old-fashioned candy store. Grab a pretzel or popcorn and meander over to Happy Days Arcade. Take a picture at the Portrait Gallery or watch an artist sketch caricatures. Sometimes people-watching on the Old Town street can be plenty entertaining in itself!

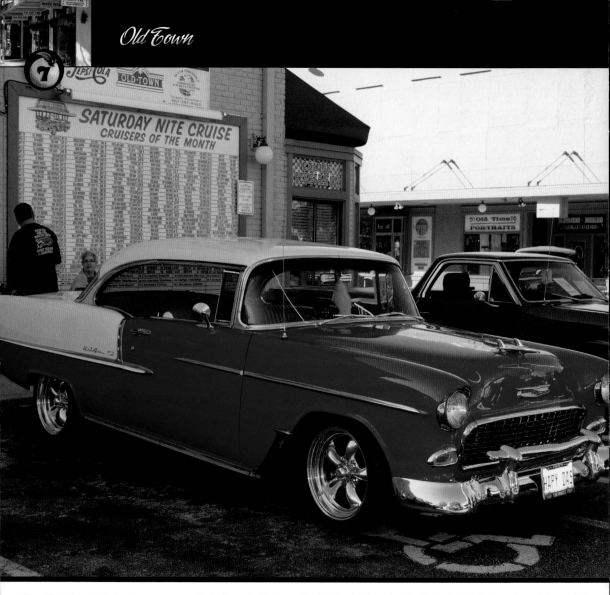

Every Saturday night, classic car owners make their way to Kissimmee for Old Town's "Saturday Nite Cruise." With their soaring tail fins and chrome-plated metalwork, the gleaming automobiles draw in crowds of spectators before the festivities even begin.

However, despite Old Town's wonderful rides, shops, and eateries, it's really the entertainment that has put this park on the map. Each week, Old Town hosts what has become the largest weekly car cruise in America. That excitement peaks every Saturday night when a live oldies band takes the stage and hundreds of show-quality classic cars parade down the street as collectors and enthusiasts celebrate the individualism and freedom that the automobile represented to mid-century America.

A time machine doesn't always have to be a futuristic looking device. Sometimes a 1950s hot rod is the vehicle of choice for a cruise down memory lane. Those looking for a traditional, mid-century amusement experience won't find one more authentic than at Old Town in Kissimmee.

8

Sam's Fun City

PENSACOLA, FLORIDA

Certain areas of the park definitely give off a California feel.

UNLIKE QUITE A FEW OF FLORIDA'S OTHER THEME PARKS, Sam's Fun City did not originate in California—though it certainly looks like it could have! With several "California-inspired" attractions, guests may even run into a celebrity or two while visiting. As the self-proclaimed "Gulf Coast Home of Rocky and Bullwinkle," characters from the famed 1960s cartoon series will frequently make an appearance here.

Located in Pensacola, Florida's westernmost city, Sam's Fun City is a fair drive from any of the state's other amusement parks. That autonomy has turned the small park into a mainstay family attraction for the coastal city. Opened in 2000, the park was an immediate success and later expanded to include Sam's Surf City, an adjoining water park in 2005.

The amusement park offers four informally themed areas—Go-Kart City, Terry Town, Yesterville and Westerville—each with a selection of rides and attractions. As one might expect, Go-Kart City features go-cart tracks—the Fun City Expressway and the Grand Prix Slick Track. Both cover a fair portion of the park grounds and pass by a few other attractions along the way. The Rookie Go-Kart Track sits just outside and offers smaller riders the chance to drive their own cart.

Terry Town offers some of history's most classic amusement rides. A Ferris wheel and the Town Center Carousel sit prominently in the center of the park just outside Sam's Fun City train station. Hop aboard the Park Train for a scenic tour of both the amusement and water parks or let the kids take the wheel on Taxi Jet or Truckin' USA.

The carousel horses stand ready for children to come take a ride.

All aboard! The park train runs the length of both Sam's Fun and Surf Cities, providing an ideal way to see all the fun at once.

Entering Go-Kart City, guests will have to make a choice between two exciting tracks. The Fun City Expressway (right) is by far the larger of the two at over 1,000 feet—complete with tunnels and a bridge. The Grand Prix Slick Track, however, is the fastest but only open to those sixteen and over with a valid driver's license.

The Ferris wheel offers the best view of the
Pensacola amusement park.

Two Yesterville attractions, Give-Peace-A-Whirl and Jitter Bug Swinger (far right) lie just beyond the railroad crossing.

Lions, dinos, and mummies ... oh my! Players will encounter some unique obstacles at the Hollywood miniature golf course.

Yesterville has a handful of aptly named attractions. The Jitter Bug Swinger—a swing attraction—and the Give-Peace-A-Whirl Tilt-A-Whirl may bring back memories of a bygone era. Pile into a horseless carriage and go for a drive with a whole family on the Antique Cars—which may find themselves putting along a few speeding go-carts as the two cross paths every now and again. Miner Mike Kids Coaster, a mini Himalayan, and Balloon Racer are all part of the area's remaining attractions.

Finally, Westerville features a handful of California-themed classics. Set sail on Bumper Boats "By-the-Bay" or get caught in the infamous Santa Ana winds aboard the Santa Ana Scrambler. "Play the Movies" at the park's eighteen-hole Hollywood miniature golf course, where each hole is a different famous film.

Like many smaller parks, admission to Sam's Fun City is free, so guests can stroll the grounds to their hearts' content. The large Crossroads Arcade also offers several alternatives to rides, including laser tag and a three story indoor Play Zone. Certainly a local favorite, this park will continue providing family fun to west-Florida and Pensacola residents for years to come.

Silver Springs' iconic Glass Bottom Boats make ready for another river excursion. Deeply rooted in Florida history, there is perhaps no attraction that better represents "old-Florida" tourism than the boat rides offered at Silver Springs.

Silver Springs

OCALA, FLORIDA

Guests peer down into the watery world below on the park's most popular attraction.

A rhesus monkey keeps an eye to sailors and passersby. Today, these accidental inhabitants are just as at home along the river as native species.

UNRIVALED IN BREATHTAKING NATURAL BEAUTY, Silver Springs is perhaps the most historic of all Florida's many tourist attractions. The invention of the glass bottom boat at Silver Springs in 1878 brought visitors in by the droves, curious to explore a once-hidden underwater world. Over the many decades that followed, Florida's endless supply of lakes and rivers would set the stage for future imitators as the state gained renown for water-based attractions and recreation.

True to its roots—which have survived nearly a century and a half now—Silver Springs' most popular attractions are still boat rides. The park's Glass Bottom Boats offer a remarkable, scenic window through the 99.8% pure artesian spring waters down to the river floor below. In the 1930s, the site began to gain notoriety as a Hollywood film hot spot and on their tour guests can still find many underwater movie props beneath the surface, which, over the years, have become homes to a wide variety of aquatic life. Film fanatics may recognize underwater locations from several James Bond movies, the popular *Sea Hunt* TV series, and even one of the most iconic horror films of all time, *Creature from the Black Lagoon*. However, sightseeing is not just confined to submerged artifacts and memorabilia. Along the banks of the Fort King River Cruise, guests will discover a Seminole Indian Village, a Florida pioneer homestead, and even wild rhesus monkeys.

The spring water is so clear it can be difficult to tell where it begins. Certainly, that clarity has been a primary factor in establishing the park as an idyllic place to observe Florida's rich, natural beauty.

Remarkably, this timeless park has not changed much over the years—remaining as "wild" as in its early days.

A park native in search of breakfast pauses along the river bank.

While monkeys are by no means native to Florida, they have occupied the land since the late 1930s when a boat ride operator brought them in to enhance his "Jungle Cruise." Unaware they were excellent swimmers, the monkeys quickly escaped and formed feral troops along the river, adding to the already rich variety of Florida wildlife found in Silver Springs.

The park offers an abundance of animal attractions and exhibits, including several shows and feeding times throughout the day, and even a petting zoo for guests' enjoyment. Guests will encounter bears, giraffes, and even extraordinarily rare white alligators as they tour the park.

A couple of parrot performers take a break before the park's free flight bird show.

While the park's river bank is home to countless native species, guests will find some rarities on Ross Allen Island. Named for the Silver Springs' herpetologist and naturalist, the island is home to a collection of reptiles, arachnids, and the park's infamous white alligators.

A Jeep Wrangler prepares for an expedition on the Wilderness Trail.

While eighty feet may not seem terribly high by today's standards, Florida's relatively flat landscape ensures that the gondolas end up amongst the treetops. As one may guess from its name, The Lighthouse Ride, the attraction also features a nighttime choreography of lights that illuminate it and the surrounding area at sundown.

Of course, the best way to discover Florida wildlife is to head where it lives. Board a Jeep Wrangler tram for a backwoods tour on the Wilderness Trail. The park's unobtrusive methods of viewing wildlife by tram and by boat provides a natural and scenic experience for all its guests. Those who wish to take in the park's vast expanse all at once are best served by The Lighthouse Ride, an eighty-foot tall gondola ride with panoramic views of the park below. For the explorer that Silver Springs uncovers in everyone, the park also offers Kids Ahoy! Playland. Here, kids will find a carousel, miniature motorboats, a play area with slides, and even a replica 1800s riverboat permanently anchored in a shallow lagoon.

For well over a century, Silver Springs has immersed visitors in the Sunshine State's natural beauty. A pioneer attraction for Florida tourism and now a living piece of state history, Silver Springs and its glass bottom boats continue to offer guests a new window on the world.

As if in tribute to the menagerie of wildlife found throughout Silver Springs, the park's carousel includes some non-traditional animals in addition to the usual horses.

In 1972, Silver Springs was designated a Registered Natural Landmark, ensuring its preservation for the enjoyment of generations to come.

A whole new park—with exciting new attractions—greets visitors to Fort Myers, Florida. *Photo provided by Zoomers Amusement Park.*

10

Zoomers
Amusement Park
FORT MYERS, FLORIDA

A welcome treat by mid-afternoon, the Bumper Boats provide a sure way to cool off. Not only is each rider equipped with their own water blaster, they'll also navigate around a waterfall and colorful buckets that pour when filled. *Photo provided by Zoomers Amusement Park.*

ZOOMERS IS A NAME NEARLY ALL FT. MYERS RESIDENTS HAVE BEEN familiar with for ages—which is surprising when you consider that this fun park is still in its infancy, having opened June 15th, 2012. While speedily-named, this park took the scenic route to opening day. However, most patrons will tell you it was well worth the wait!

Development on Zoomers Amusement Park actually began in 2002. After some delays—including damage from Hurricanes Charley in 2004 and Wilma in 2005, it looked as though construction was nearing the finish line. However, the road to opening day proved to stretch on much further. By 2007, all construction on the nearly completed amusement park screeched to a halt. For several years the park sat dormant and anxious Ft. Myers residents began to doubt that this roadside tease would ever make it past the starting line. However, Zoomers' luck finally changed in 2011, when the park was sold at auction and a new owner hit the gas to get the park back on track. After just one year of renovation and rebuilding, the new park opened following a decade of stop-and-go development.

Drivers take a hairpin turn on one of the park's popular go-cart tracks. *Photo provided by Zoomers Amusement Park.*

While guests will find rides both in and out of the midway section, those located within are generally meant for younger riders. Parents have the option to enjoy select midway rides along with their children, or relax under a shady gazebo while the kids ride over and over again. *Photo provided by Zoomers Amusement Park.*

Riders have a laugh on the Tilt-A-Whirl. *Photo provided by Zoomers Amusement Park.*

Charismatic tikis welcome guests to Voodoo Island Miniature Golf. *Photo provided by Zoomers Amusement Park.*

The arcade has lots of fun family games that can be enjoyed rain or shine. *Photo provided by Zoomers Amusement Park.*

Trophies come in all shapes and sizes; pick yours out at the Winners Circle prize center. *Photo provided by Zoomers Amusement Park.*

Visitors to this eighteen-acre amusement park have hours of fun to look forward to. The park's midway offers a variety of rides—quite a few meant exclusively for their youngest guests. While Chair Swing, Under the Sea, and Gorilla Show don't allow adult riders, there are plenty of family rides that guests can enjoy together. Pirate Ship and Frog Hopper both offer mild thrills while the park's family roller coaster, tilt-a-whirl, bumper boats, and the mini-toot train round out the rides.

For older guests looking to hit the throttle a little harder, the park's namesake go-cart tracks won't disappoint. The Road Go-Cart Track is appropriate for all young and old drivers who meet the height requirement, but those looking for a true challenge might prefer the Slick Track. Thrill-seekers daring enough to take on this slippery speedway should note that the track is only open to licensed drivers.

Families who prefer activities outside the rides and go-carts have quite a few other options to choose from. The eighteen-hole voodoo miniature golf course will have them trekking through a rain forest of tropical plants, tikis, and lush scenery while being serenaded by jungle animal sounds. With a large arcade, mini-bowling, and prize center, there's a good time to be had by everyone.

Ft. Myers—the City of Palms—has long been a recreation destination. Lining the Gulf of Mexico, vacation goers on their way to the beach and its many water activities have taken pleasure in the wonderful fishing, boat tours, golfing, and shopping that the region has to offer. Today, however, those delightfully Floridian recreations have an exciting new attraction as well. And while it may have been slow out of the gate, you can bet that this amusement park will have guests speeding on in for decades down the road.

Known for its amazing marine life shows and
attractions, SeaWorld operates its largest multi-park
experience in Orlando, Florida.

11

SeaWorld Parks and
Entertainment, Orlando

ORLANDO, FLORIDA

Snorkelers navigate The Grand Reef, one of Discovery Cove's large snorkeling pools. Here, visitors will encounter thousands of colorful fish, rays, and even reef sharks kept safely behind glass. *Photo provided by SeaWorld. ©SeaWorld Parks & Entertainment, Inc. All rights reserved. Reproduced by permission.*

SeaWorld's immersive oceanic encounter, Discovery Cove, welcomes guests to a new world of interaction and fun.

BILLED AS A PLACE "WHERE WORLDS CONNECT," SeaWorld has become famous for inviting guests to explore the wonders of life in our oceans. On a planet where more than two-thirds of the surface is covered in water, the innumerable and fascinating creatures below the surface make all SeaWorld parks a place of wonderful discovery.

Like many Florida-based theme parks, SeaWorld opened its first park in California but later expanded to other regions. Also, akin to other major theme park companies, SeaWorld now operates its largest tourist attraction in Orlando—with three unique venues. Busch Gardens Tampa Bay, a sister-park to SeaWorld Orlando, is also just over an hour away.

SeaWorld Orlando, the company's first Orlando-based park, opened in 1973. Like the original SeaWorld park in San Diego, it offers guests a chance to get up close to marine life—as well as a chance to experience a wide variety of marine-life themed thrills and attractions. Since 2000, however, SeaWorld has expanded into new parks—all with the goal of bringing guests closer to our oceans and the captivating life within them. Discovery Cove, an entirely new tourist park concept, features a completely immersive

Offering a superb selection of slides, Aquatica has something for leisure-leaning guests or those predisposed to be daredevils—like the eight-person Taumata Racer at the far left.

Opened in 2008, Aquatica was an immediate success. As a company renowned for world class, water-based entertainment, SeaWorld's much anticipated water park was a natural fit.

snorkeling experience. A "reservation-only" park, Discovery Cove caps the number of daily visitors to 1,000. Equipment rentals, a reserved dolphin swim experience, even food and beverages are included in the package—as well as admission to another of SeaWorld's nearby parks for the days following. While the park does not offer rides, guests visiting Discovery Cove will appreciate that the 1,000 guest cap eliminates the crowds typically found at other parks, making the beaches and reefs a perfect environment to relax and explore.

Water park enthusiasts will also enjoy SeaWorld's water park, Aquatica. Inspired by the South Pacific, Aquatica delivers on its promise to "plunge guests through the sea"—literally. The park's signature attraction, Dolphin Plunge, features two clear tube slides that take guests on a thrilling ride beneath the surface and through a dolphin pool. Guests visiting the park will enjoy the thrills of a traditional water park, but reinvented with a twist from the world's most popular marine life park.

SeaWorld's Orlando parks are all centrally located—fifteen minutes from Orlando International Airport. Those looking to explore more of Central Florida's world-famous attractions will relish in the fact that they are just twenty minutes from no less than fifteen different theme, amusement, and water parks, spanning out in all directions.

Florida's water-loving flamingos make perfect paddle boats at SeaWorld Orlando.

Coral reefs are undersea hotels filled with amazing animals that constantly check in and out. As manager of the world's most amazing hotels (and restaurants), your everyday actions count -- don't trash where you splash, support sustainable seafood and check into SeaWorld.org.

SeaWorld's conservation efforts are prevalent in the parks; however, those efforts are just the beginning. In 2003, the company launched The SeaWorld & Busch Gardens Conservation Fund, a non-profit foundation aimed at providing guests a direct way to get involved with wildlife conservation around the globe.

At home in SeaWorld's Manta Aquarium, these tropical residents often teach more about oceanic life than would ever be possible in the classroom—even if they're not swimming in schools!

SeaWorld has long been committed to driving conservation efforts around the globe. While supporting research, animal rescue and rehabilitation are certainly key aspects of their mission, educating visitors about the natural world and its non-human inhabitants may be SeaWorld's greatest accomplishment. Since the first SeaWorld park opened in 1964, SeaWorld has inspired guests to learn and study animals that few humans would ever interact with otherwise. The wonders of our oceans are many—SeaWorld parks invite guests into the blue, and into the vast worlds of discovery beneath the surface.

one Ocean

12

SeaWorld Orlando

ORLANDO, FLORIDA

A harbor lighthouse welcomes guests to SeaWorld Orlando. *Photo provided by SeaWorld. ©SeaWorld Parks & Entertainment, Inc. All rights reserved. Reproduced by permission.*

While certainly renowned for its oceanic wildlife, this colorful park is home to more than just sea creatures.

FLORIDA HAS ALWAYS HAD A UNIQUE FASCINATION WITH MARINE LIFE, so when SeaWorld Orlando opened in 1973, it was a tremendous success. Over the years, SeaWorld Orlando has gained distinction as the world's most popular marine-life theme park.

Unlike many other big-name theme parks, SeaWorld is not broken up into lands—but rather, features individually themed attractions, as well as some select themed areas. All park attractions, however, have some connection to the sea.

SeaWorld Orlando offers three major thrill rides—Journey to Atlantis is an exciting water coaster that narrates guests through a legend of the lost island civilization. The attraction begins calmly, with a boat ride through the colorful canals of Atlantis. But the ambiance quickly changes when a deceitful siren reveals her true form and guests are sent hurtling to the waters below as the ride changes into a hybrid boat flume and roller coaster. Kraken, a coaster inspired by another legend of the sea, takes guests on a ride as wild as the sea monster itself. The park's last major thrill attraction, Manta, begins in a quiet seaside village.

iders prepare for a drenching drop in what appears to be the finale of ourney to Atlantis. Moments later, however, guests will find their boat scending once again as they take on one final splashdown with the siren.

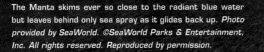

The Manta skims ever so close to the radiant blue water but leaves behind only sea spray as it glides back up. *Photo provided by SeaWorld. ©SeaWorld Parks & Entertainment, Inc. All rights reserved. Reproduced by permission.*

Prior to boarding Manta, guests will be immersed in a stunning underwater world. With hundreds of rays and even a giant Pacific octopus, this may be the first attraction where guests complain the line moves too quickly!

As guests wind through the queue, they'll discover mosaics and astounding aquariums throughout, dedicated to the ocean's largest ray. The queue leading up to the ride itself is so popular, SeaWorld has even made it accessible to guests who choose not to ride the coaster so they too can experience the grace and beauty of the rays as they fly through the ocean like birds. Appropriately, once thrill-seekers reach the station they'll board a flying coaster, which will send them through the skies, and then skimming so close to the water a few guests may get wet.

As with Manta, SeaWorld tries to incorporate animal encounters into many of its attractions. Wild Arctic Ride, a popular motion simulator trek through the frozen north, also includes a walkthrough animal exhibit with walruses, polar bears, and even beluga whales. However, those who prefer to forego the rides altogether will enjoy Dolphin Cove, Shark Encounter, or Pacific Point Preserve, which offer a chance to get up close with a variety of oceanic and marine life animals.

An exciting "jet-helicopter" ride through skies and seas, Wild Arctic Ride will have passengers racing to Base Station before an arctic storm hits.

Two curious sea lions wait patiently for handouts. At Pacific Point Preserve, guests have the opportunity to feed these playful personalities if they so choose.

Throughout the day, kids will encounter all sorts of fuzzy friends at SeaWorld Orlando. But no matter how many they find in the park, there are always plenty more looking for a home!

Perhaps SeaWorld's greatest claim to fame, however, is its inspiring shows. Throughout the park, guests will encounter a wide variety of stadiums and theaters, each designed for different types of performances. The park's killer whale venue, "Shamu Stadium," is one of the most spectacular. Because most shows feature animal stars, SeaWorld only offers a few daily showtimes for each program. Guests are advised to arrive early since the stadiums will often fill up.

Say "Ahoy" to fun! Shamu's Happy Harbor has all sorts of rides and activities for kids.

Apart from the shows and animal encounters, SeaWorld also offers a plethora of kid-friendly attractions. At Shamu's Happy Harbor, families will enjoy rides on Swishy Fishies, Jazzy Jellies, and of course the Shamu Express, a mild coaster named after SeaWorld's most famous killer whale. With the addition of a completely immersive "Antarctica" experience area in 2013, SeaWorld Orlando continues to lead the way in satisfying the world's unending curiosity and fascination with marine life.

For generations, visitors have discovered new worlds at SeaWorld Orlando. Certainly that won't change any time soon for this beloved marine-life park.

For more than a century, Universal has been a symbol for world-class entertainment. Guests can rest assured that they will find nothing less at the Universal Orlando® Resort. *Photo provided by Universal. © 2012 Universal Orlando Resort. All rights reserved.*

13

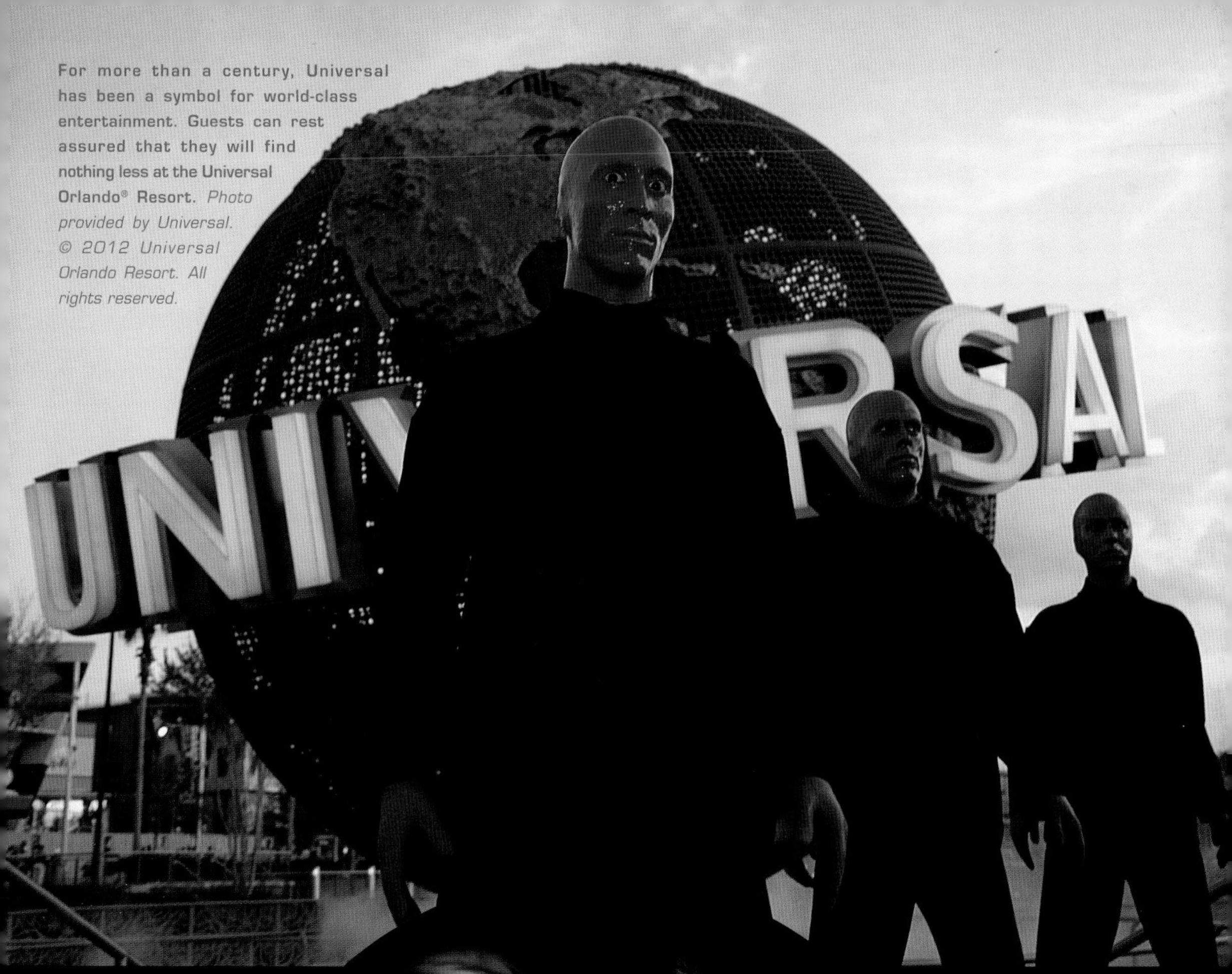

Universal Orlando Resort

ORLANDO, FLORIDA

With so much to do, guests should plan on spending several days at the Universal Orlando® Resort.

Of course, at a resort themed around movie magic, a movie theater is an absolute must.

UNIVERSAL HAS BECOME ONE OF THE HOTTEST NAMES IN THE THEME park world—and for good reason. As America's oldest film studio still in continuous production, it offers unparalleled theme park attractions that immerse guests into the world of movies. Now operating theme parks around the globe, those looking for the pinnacle "big-screen" experience need look no further than Orlando.

The Universal Orlando® Resort is the company's largest tourist attraction, made up of two theme parks—Universal Studios Florida® and Universal's Islands of Adventure®—as well as the famed water park, Wet 'n Wild®. Originally envisioned as a single theme park that would allow guests to "ride the movies," Universal Studios Florida® first opened in 1990. However, its popularity necessitated plans for expansion almost immediately and by the early 2000s, the one park had been transformed into the world famous theme park resort we know today.

Guests staying "on location" have their choice between three hotels, each with its own attitude. The Hard Rock Hotel® showcases the glitz and glamour of the rock 'n' roll industry while the Loews Portofino Bay Hotel and the Loews Royal Pacific Hotel offer luxurious Italian and South Seas experiences respectively. Those looking for additional shopping, dining, and entertainment experiences will find them at Universal CityWalk® Orlando, a retail district conveniently located just outside both theme parks.

On their way to the theme parks, guests will pass through Universal's CityWalk® Orlando, a retail district that packs as much excitement as the parks themselves.

Enjoy nightly entertainment and even get in on the action; Citywalk's Rising Star is the ultimate karaoke experience for those bold enough to take the stage! *Photo provided by Universal. © 2012 Universal Orlando Resort. All rights reserved.*

The Latin Quarter™ features flavorfully inspired dishes from Florida's southern neighbors. With colorful and vibrant nightlife, patrons can also enjoy live music and dancing. *Photo provided by Universal. © 2012 Universal Orlando Resort. All rights reserved.*

While everything at the resort is in fairly close proximity, there is a good deal of ground to cover. Those looking to experience everything should plan on staying for a few days. The vibrant nightlife also allows the resort to reinvent itself each evening; night owls will appreciate that Universal CityWalk® stays open until 2:00 AM, 365 days a year. The Universal Orlando® Resort is also conveniently located in the heart of central Florida, twenty minutes or less from other nearby theme parks and Orlando International Airport.

Although guests visiting central Florida can enjoy warm weather year round, Universal has also become famous for its seasonal celebrations as well. The resort puts on a prominent concert series during the summer months featuring some of the biggest names in the music industry as well as Mardi Gras parades in the springtime and a holiday event during the winter. However, the most famous of Universal's seasonal attractions takes place in the fall—the resort's Halloween Horror Nights®. The award-winning event first debuted in 1991 and quickly became recognized as the nation's premier Halloween haunt. In keeping with the movie theme, guests may stumble across some of Hollywood's most famous horrors while trekking through the studios.

While the resort tends to draw fewer families with very young children than other nearby attractions, Universal Orlando® Resort truly does offer something for everyone. The spectacular Wizarding World of Harry Potter™ at Universal's Islands of Adventure® has also recently transformed the resort into a Mecca for wizards and "muggles" alike. Those looking for an immersive "movie-magic" experience will find the blockbuster bash they're looking for at the Universal Orlando® Resort.

Seasonal celebrations, like Mardi Gras, keep the resort filled with ever-changing festivities.

14

Universal Studios Florida

ORLANDO, FLORIDA

Universal Orlando's Horror Make-Up Show provides a comical look at some of Hollywood's horror film effects. It is one of the few park attractions that has been operating since opening day.

As America's oldest film studio, Universal has deep Hollywood roots. Naturally, guests can expect to find some whimsically recreated landmarks while exploring the park.

UNLIKE ITS SISTER PARK, UNIVERSAL STUDIOS HOLLYWOOD—which operated as a Hollywood Studio long before it first offered rides—Universal Studios Florida® was envisioned as a theme park from the get-go. Because of that, the Florida park offers attractions that allow guests to "ride the movies," whereas its California counterpart focuses much more on showing how movies are made. This was fairly unfamiliar territory for the movie-making juggernauts, and Universal Studios Florida® spent nearly a decade in development before it finally opened on June 7th, 1990.

The park features six lands, all themed to various aspects of movie-making. Throughout, guests will find a good deal of film memorabilia amassed over more than a century of big screen entertainment. Many attractions at the park were developed with the blockbuster creators and actors reprising their roles, which makes each experience all-the-more authentic.

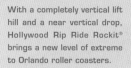

With a completely vertical lift hill and a near vertical drop, Hollywood Rip Ride Rockit® brings a new level of extreme to Orlando roller coasters.

Each lap bar features a built in audio control panel where guests choose between several genres before selecting their personal soundtrack for the ride.

Universal Studios Florida® brings quite a bit of interactivity to its attractions. Those looking for their chance in the limelight can catch their big break at Disaster!℠ A Major Motion Picture Ride … Starring YOU!

Careen through the darkness where surprises haunt every turn. Be sure to remain seated— this coaster ends with an unexpected twist!

San Francisco, I presume? As a city that's known for its diverse cuisine, guests can find some great seafood here—as well as decadent pastries.

The park opens onto Production Central; but unlike many other theme parks, which only offer stores and restaurants along the entry way, guests are greeted by several exciting attractions including Hollywood Rip Ride Rockit®. As one of Florida's most exciting roller coasters—167 feet tall and reaching speeds of 65 mph—Hollywood Rip Ride Rockit® boasts one very unique feature: it lets guests control their airwaves. With audio equipment installed into each headrest on the coaster, guests select their own high-energy soundtrack before the ride begins—which rocks the coaster as soon as it leaves the station.

From Production Central, guests can continue onto lands inspired by three popular movie settings—New York, San Francisco, and Hollywood. New York features the popular Revenge of the Mummy® indoor roller coaster, housed inside an ominous Museum of Antiquities. Avoid fireballs, scarab beetles, and a supernatural curse that haunts the attraction. Film critics, however, may prefer the Delancey Street Preview Center, where qualified

guests will get a chance to view and rate a brand new Universal film or show currently under network consideration. In San Francisco, guests can participate as "extras" in the hilarious Disaster!^{SM} A Major Motion Picture Ride ... Starring YOU, or put themselves to the test at the most extreme audience participation show ever, Fear Factor Live. Hollywood offers a little more glamour—and gore. Enjoy a tribute to first-lady of television, Lucille Ball, or discover the secret techniques Hollywood make-up artists use on the silver screen at Universal Orlando's Horror Make-Up Show.

The park's final two lands offer some exciting family attractions. At World Expo, protect the planet from aliens on the interactive MEN IN BLACK™ Alien Attack™, or—at The Simpsons Ride™—hop on a "questionable-at-best," new ride at Krusty the Clown's new theme park. Finally, Woody Woodpecker's Kidzone® offers great shows and rides for the younger crowd. Meet TV's most popular purple dinosaur, Barney, or head through two

Home to Universal Studios' theme park mascot, Woody Woodpecker, fun-seekers will also find Curious George, Barney, and a slew of other popular children's characters at Woody Woodpecker's KidZone®.

Woody Woodpecker's Nuthouse Coaster® is a ride as wacky as the woodpecker himself!

Even all the way across the country, the streets of Hollywood are very much alive at Universal Studios Florida®.

interactive playgrounds inspired by Curious George and the popular cartoon mouse, Fievel. Young and old will both enjoy a flying bicycle ride through the popular Steven Spielberg film, *E.T.*, on E.T. Adventure®.

Whether guests are looking for shows, rides, or something new altogether, they'll be able to find it at Universal Studios Florida®—all wrapped up in the excitement that only a century of movie-making can bring.

15
Universal's Islands of Adventure

ORLANDO, FLORIDA

Universal's Islands of Adventure® offers an exciting voyage for anyone daring enough to set sail!

THE IDEA FOR A SECOND UNIVERSAL ORLANDO THEME PARK SURFACED
as little as a year after Universal Studios Florida® finally opened. Concepts for a "Cartoon World" were drawn up over the next couple years but it wasn't until 1993—following Universal's blockbuster film, Jurassic Park®—that plans for a new park were announced to the public. The park's original theme was reworked, and exploration and adventure became the foundation for all the park attractions.

Universal's Islands of Adventure® opened May 28th, 1999, and currently offers seven "islands" inspired by exciting and imaginative locations across the literary world, that later found themselves on the big-screen. Port of Entry® functions as the park's main entrance. From there, a prominent lighthouse beams outward to the remaining six islands; and guides explorers to and from the park gates.

Keep a sharp eye out for one-of-a-kind artifacts. There's treasure a plenty in this gem of a theme park.

Pharos Lighthouse welcomes adventures to the many exciting "Islands" within. *Photo provided by Universal. © 2012 Universal Orlando Resort. All rights reserved.*

The park features three "cartoon" islands expanding out from the Port of Entry®. The first, Seuss Landing™, retells popular children's stories from literature's most famous "Doctor." There's a lot on this plot—the perfect spot for a tot. From One Fish, Two Fish, Red Fish, Blue Fish™ to The Cat in the Hat™, families will enjoy rides that they can all do together. Marvel Super Hero Island® on the other hand, immerses guests in a comic book world. With award-winning attractions like The Incredible Hulk coaster® and The Amazing Adventures of Spider-Man®, fans can experience the thrill of fighting evil alongside some of the world's most popular heroes. Finally, Toon Lagoon® showcases characters from around the cartoon world, all brought together in one chaotic and whacky island. With shops and restaurants inspired by the Sunday "funnies," Toon Lagoon® also features some wild water rides. Board a river raft with Popeye or hop in a log and save the day on Dudley Do-Right's Ripshaw Falls®—one of the world's most popular log flumes. Curses—foiled again!

THE CAT IN THE HAT

The whimsical world of Dr. Seuss comes to life at Seuss Landing™. *Photo provided by Universal. © 2012 Universal Orlando Resort. All rights reserved.*

Towering above Marvel Super Hero Island®, guests will encounter some larger than life attractions here including The Incredible Hulk Coaster®. In addition to turning things big and green, gamma rays can apparently produce some gargantuan thrills! *Photo provided by Universal. © 2012 Universal Orlando Resort. All rights reserved.*

The Lost Continent® is an island of mystery and legend—as well as fabled good food. Those looking for a full service dining experience need look no further than Mythos Restaurant®, a place of delicious enchantment.

Heading out from the cartoon worlds, guests will encounter some even more adventurous islands. The Lost Continent® transports guests into far off and mythical experiences. Witness spectacular feats at The Eighth Voyage of Sinbad® Stunt Show, or tour remnants of the sea god's lost temple at Poseidon's Fury®. In Jurassic Park®, guests can experience the blockbuster film like it was meant to be experienced—as a theme park. Embark on an expedition through lost worlds on Jurassic Park River Adventure®, but be careful—not all dinosaurs are herbivores! Soar through the skies on the Pteranodon Flyers® or explore a prehistoric playground at Camp Jurassic®.

Steaming into the park in 2010, the Hogwarts Express™ welcomes "muggles" to Hogsmeade™ and The Wizarding World of Harry Potter™. *Photo provided by Universal. © 2012 Universal Orlando Resort. All rights reserved. HARRY POTTER, characters, names and related indicia are trademarks of and © Warner Bros. Entertainment Inc. Harry Potter Publishing Rights © JKR. (s12)*

Those on their way to Hagrid's hut may enjoy a ride on Flight of the Hippogriff™, a milder alternative to the exciting Dragon Challenge™ dueling roller coasters. *Photo provided by Universal. © 2012 Universal Orlando Resort. All rights reserved. HARRY POTTER, characters, names and related indicia are trademarks of and © Warner Bros. Entertainment Inc. Harry Potter Publishing Rights © JKR. (s12)*

Universal's immersive recreations of literary and big-screen masterpieces have made Universal's Islands of Adventure® one of the world's most popular theme parks ... and home to some of the greatest stories ever told. *Photo provided by Universal. © 2012 Universal Orlando Resort. All rights reserved. HARRY POTTER, characters, names and related indicia are trademarks of and © Warner Bros. Entertainment Inc. Harry Potter Publishing Rights © JKR. (s12)*

The park's seventh and final island, The Wizarding World of Harry Potter™, opened to rave reviews in 2010—at least in the "muggle" world. Have a glass of Butterbeer™ at the Three Broomsticks™, or stock up on magic pranks at Zonko's™. Enjoy Bertie Bott's Every Flavour Beans™ or Chocolate Frogs™ at Honeydukes™. Find your wand at Ollivanders™. Wander the grounds and corridors of Hogwarts™ at Harry Potter and the Forbidden Journey™ and take a breathtaking broomstick ride above the castle.

With so much to explore, those charting a course for Universal's Islands of Adventure® will discover that the voyage itself was a treasure worth seeking.

Florida's scenic waterways make traveling by boat not only efficient, but also a fantastic way to enjoy panoramic views of Disney's many diverse venues.
Disney elements ©Disney Enterprises, Inc.

16

Walt Disney World Resort

LAKE BUENA VISTA, FLORIDA

As they explore the more than 30,000 acres that make up the Walt Disney World® Resort, guests will find new adventures around every bend. Perhaps the best way to see everything is by balloon. Characters in Flight, operated by Aérophile, offers a breathtaking 400 foot view of the entire resort. *Disney elements ©Disney Enterprises, Inc.*

IN THE WORLD OF TRAVEL, comparisons are often made to the world's top tourism icons. Some theme parks may claim to have "one of the top family attractions in the world" or boast that they offer more rides than competitors. However, when it comes to the world's top theme park resort, it's difficult to make a genuine comparison.

The Walt Disney World® Resort opened its first park, Magic Kingdom® Park, in 1971. Since then, it has expanded to offer three additional theme parks—Epcot®, Disney's Hollywood Studios®, and Disney's Animal Kingdom®—transforming Disney's central Florida attraction into the most visited recreational resort in the entire world. At nearly 50 square miles, it's also the largest. Each of Disney's four theme parks rank in world's "top ten most visited" with the original, Magic Kingdom® Park, claiming global top honors with roughly seventeen million annual guests.

As the world's most visited entertainment resort, the Walt Disney World® Resort welcomes tens of millions of guests to its unique magic every year. *Disney elements ©Disney Enterprises, Inc.*

Other unique entertainment venues include DisneyQuest® Indoor Interactive Theme Park, an expansive five-story interactive gaming experience located in Downtown Disney®. *Disney elements ©Disney Enterprises, Inc.*

Outside the theme parks—which are covered individually in the next four chapters—the resort also operates the world's two most popular water parks, Disney's Typhoon Lagoon and Disney's Blizzard Beach—both inspired by Florida's unpredictable weather. For the culinary connoisseur or shopping aficionado, the world-famous Downtown Disney® district offers unmatched retail and dining options, punctuated with a nightlife featuring world-class performance acts. For the sports fan, the ESPN Wide World of Sports Complex hosts numerous athletic events each year, both amateur and professional. If that weren't enough, the resort also maintains a plethora of pristine golf courses, a turn-of-the-century style boardwalk, and roughly thirty themed resort hotels, each with its own allure. When visiting the Walt Disney World® Resort, guests of all ages can be sure that regardless of their preferences, they will find much to delight them throughout their trip.

Throughout the resort, guests can choose between hundreds of retail shops to find the perfect souvenirs for their trip. Step into the World of Disney® store for the ultimate Disney shopping experience. *Disney elements ©Disney Enterprises, Inc.*

The endless courses make the Walt Disney World® Resort a paradise for golf enthusiasts. Those looking for a quicker and perhaps more "kid-friendly" game may prefer the resort's themed miniature golf courses. *Disney elements ©Disney Enterprises, Inc.*

A trip to the Walt Disney World® Resort is best enjoyed over several days. The vast resort is well served by an excellent transportation system, and guests staying on-site will appreciate that when they park their cars, there's no need to drive for the remainder of their vacation. An army of buses, as well as fleets of monorails and boats traverse the roads and waterways between the parks, venues, and hotels, giving guests more time to relax and enjoy their stay. Those planning to visit other destinations in the Orlando area, will also appreciate that the resort is located conveniently along I-4 and US 192, just twenty miles from Orlando International Airport and a stone's throw from the world-famous International Drive.

With countless resort hotels to choose from, guests can enjoy immersive stays in Polynesian-, Caribbean-, and even Wilderness-themed retreats. Disney's Grand Floridian Resort & Spa seen here is inspired by Victorian era beach resorts that dotted Florida's coast during the early twentieth century. *Disney elements ©Disney Enterprises, Inc.*

For many, a trip to the Walt Disney World® Resort is a once in a lifetime event. It's a chance to meet childhood heroes and enjoy stories that have been passed down for generations. So whether it's a dream family vacation, a romantic honeymoon, or the celebration of an important milestone, Walt Disney World® Resort is a place where magic still exists.

For guest convenience, Disney offers a variety of complimentary travel options to get from one site to another. The Walt Disney World Monorail System provides high speed transportation between Magic Kingdom® Park, Epcot®, and a selection of resort hotels. *Disney elements ©Disney Enterprises, Inc.*

Once guests enter the park and step onto Main Street, U.S.A.®, they are instantly transported back to the early 1900s, and into Walt Disney's own boyhood memories.
Disney elements ©Disney Enterprises, Inc.

17

Magic Kingdom Park

LAKE BUENA VISTA, FLORIDA

Situated in the center of Magic Kingdom® Park, Cinderella Castle has become a world-renowned icon for the imagination and enchantment that make up the world's most visited theme park.
Disney elements ©Disney Enterprises, Inc.

For a bear of very little brain, the unending search for "hunny" can lead to many exciting adventures. *Disney elements ©Disney. Based on the "Winnie the Pooh" works by A.A. Milne and E.H. Shepard.*

AS THE MOST VISITED THEME PARK IN THE WORLD, with roughly seventeen million guests a year, it's no surprise that Magic Kingdom® Park is often mistakenly referred to as "Disneyworld" on its own. Inspired by the original Disneyland® Park in California, Magic Kingdom® Park opened on October 1st, 1971, as the Walt Disney World® Resort's first theme park.

The park's six themed lands pay tribute to important periods in history, retell age-old stories and fairy tales, and envision a new future altogether. With the exception of Liberty Square, each land was personally developed by Walt Disney for Disneyland in 1955.

Main Street, U.S.A.®, inspired by Walt Disney's boyhood town of Marceline, Missouri, at the turn of the twentieth century, serves as an entry plaza to the park's five additional lands. Horse drawn streetcars and horseless carriages make their way up and down the lively street—past five and dime shops, parlors, and eateries. Once guests reach the park's central hub, their next land is just steps away.

Swiss Family Treehouse, a walk-through Adventureland® attraction, offers a whimsical and inventive look into what life might be like for a family shipwrecked on a tropical island. *Disney elements ©Disney Enterprises, Inc.*

Filled with laughin', splashin', satisfactual fun, Splash Mountain® will delight everyone seeking to add a little more "Zip-a-Dee-Doo-Dah" to their day. *Disney elements ©Disney Enterprises, Inc.*

Those with an eye for adventure will enjoy a trip back in time to far regions of the globe. Set sail with Captain Jack Sparrow in pursuit of an elusive treasure map on Pirates of the Caribbean®, one of the most popular theme park rides ever built. Embark on a river voyage through dense wilderness aboard Adventureland® area's most iconic attraction, Jungle Cruise. But guests shouldn't spend too long abroad—there's plenty more adventure to be had on America's own soil.

Frontierland®, themed to America's Old West, boasts several "don't miss" attractions: Splash Mountain®, a sing-along log flume ride, drops guests five stories south into the Uncle Remus folk tales. Tom Sawyer Island offers a free-roaming maze of bridges, caves, and uncharted territory.

The high seas await—but keep a sharp eye out! Adventure, treasure, and pirates are hiding around every cove! *Disney elements ©Disney Enterprises, Inc.*

Inspired by some of Mark Twain's most
popular novels—guests are free to explore the
world of Tom Sawyer in Frontierland®. *Disney
elements ©Disney Enterprises, Inc.*

Always reinventing itself, discover the world of tomorrow, today! *Disney elements ©Disney Enterprises, Inc.*

When ready to head back to civilization, the park's Liberty Square can offer an easy transition. Guests can tour The Hall of Presidents for an inspiring spectacle, or traverse The Haunted Mansion® with expired specters.

Tomorrowland® will delight those with their eyes on the future. Board a shuttle for the far reaches of the universe on Space Mountain®, the Walt Disney World® Resort's first roller coaster, or join the Galactic Alliance and rid the galaxy of evil aboard Buzz Lightyear's Space Ranger Spin®. Help power the city of Monstropolis with newly discovered "Laugh energy," or pilot a rocket aboard the Astro Orbiter®.

And finally, Walt Disney's favorite kingdom of all, Fantasyland®, offers children the chance to meet storybook characters and live their adventures as well. Recently expanded to twice the size of the original Fantasyland®, visitors can now enjoy a ride through the seven dwarfs' mine, or board a clam to head under the sea with Princess Ariel.

Built for the world's fair in 1964, Walt Disney's Carousel of Progress continues to turn a half century later at Magic Kingdom® Park. This ageless attraction takes guests on a journey showing how electricity and technology have improved our lives over the past 100 years. Above, travelers can be spotted aboard the Tomorrowland® Transit Authority PeopleMover, which provides an idealized and scenic form of future transportation. *Disney elements ©Disney Enterprises, Inc.*

With the recent discovery that laughter is ten times more powerful than scream energy, join Mike Wazowski for a hilarious performance in Monstropolis' first comedy club. *Monsters, Inc. Laugh Floor is inspired by Disney®Pixar's film Monsters, Inc. Disney/Pixar elements ©Disney Enterprises, Inc./Pixar.*

Magic Kingdom® Park—like Disneyland® Park in California—was envisioned as a place where families could have fun together, and imagination would always be alive. A charming combination of old and new, it sets the standard in the Sunshine State.

Join in on the loopy, loony fun of an "un-birthday" celebration at the Mad Tea Party in Fantasyland®. *Disney elements ©Disney Enterprises, Inc.*

For decades, Disney's dedication to storytelling has made the theme park "The Most Magical Place On Earth." *Disney elements ©Disney Enterprises, Inc.*

In Future World, prior to boarding on Mission: SPACE®, riders will be broken into groups of four and each given an assignment as they pilot their shuttle to Mars. *Disney elements ©Disney Enterprises, Inc.*

18

Epcot

LAKE BUENA VISTA, FLORIDA

A Viking welcomes guests to the Norway pavilion at World Showcase. *Disney elements ©Disney Enterprises, Inc.*

Since the beginning of time, humans have relied on the land they inhabit for a variety of resources. Discover what the future may hold, and how creative new developments will improve the farms of tomorrow. *Disney elements ©Disney Enterprises, Inc.*

WALT DISNEY'S LAST GREAT PROJECT, EPCOT®, was originally envisioned as a futuristic city with a population of 20,000, not a theme park. Previously an all-caps acronym for Experimental Prototype Community of Tomorrow (sometimes Experimental Prototype City of Tomorrow), EPCOT was the primary reason Disney purchased the unprecedented 30,000 acres of land that would eventually become the Walt Disney World® Resort.

Sadly, Walt Disney passed away before his dream was realized, but the ideas of EPCOT were not forgotten. On October 1st, 1982, a new theme park experience, inspired by Walt's creative vision, finally opened to the public. With a theme of unity through technology and international harmony, the park features two central lands: Future World and World Showcase. At more than twice the size of Magic Kingdom® Park, guests hoping to experience everything this unique park has to offer should plan for a busy day—or split the day's activities into two.

The centerpiece of Epcot®, Spaceship Earth transports time-travelers through an incredibly beautiful and enriching history of human communication. *Disney elements* *©Disney Enterprises, Inc.*

Where does energy come from? How can we harness other sustainable sources? Head back in time with Ellen DeGeneres to unearth the past ... and plan for the future! *Disney elements ©Disney Enterprises, Inc.*

Future World, a land quite literally "driven" by new ideas, invites guests to explore some of the exciting scientific frontiers facing our globe today. Pilot a shuttle for Mars on Mission: SPACE®, or take the wheel from a crash test dummy on Test Track® Presented by Chevrolet®, two of Future World's most exciting attractions. Learn about breakthroughs in agriculture aboard Living with the Land, or exciting prospects for renewable energy on Ellen's Energy Adventure. Take a trip back in time to understand mankind's accomplishments, and see how new inventions continue to shape our day-to-day lives on Spaceship Earth. Throughout Future World, guests are invited to learn and imagine what will make the world a better place for generations to come.

Imagination!, one of Future World's many colorful venues, offers several attractions that will engage the mind and delight the senses. *Disney elements ©Disney Enterprises, Inc.*

The Seas with Nemo & Friends is another great Future World pavilion—where fish are friends, not food! Embark on an undersea quest to find Nemo or chat with everyone's favorite surfer turtle, Crush. *The Seas with Nemo & Friends attraction is inspired by the Disney Pixar film Finding Nemo. Disney/Pixar elements ©Disney Enterprises, Inc./Pixar.*

World Showcase stays true to each nation's culture, bringing in performers from around the world to represent their country. *Disney elements ©Disney Enterprises, Inc.*

Though they don't appear on the park map, some pavilions offer a museum of sorts, which provide an enriching look into the history and culture of the countries they showcase. *Disney elements ©Disney Enterprises, Inc.*

World Showcase offers a trip around the world, with pavilions hosted by eleven different countries. Adding to the authenticity of the experience, each of Disney's cast members is actually from the host pavilion they represent. Guests will enjoy boat trips through the history and culture of Mexico and Norway, as well as enlightening films by China, the United States, France, and Canada. Germany, Italy, Japan, Morocco, and the United Kingdom offer a variety of exhibits, and all eleven nations redefine "theme park food" by offering inspired dishes from regional cuisines. Many "foodies" will also enjoy the fact that each pavilion proudly stocks local wines and beers brewed by their host country.

SPIRITED BEASTS

FROM ANCIENT STORIES TO ANIME STARS

For centuries, heroic animals and magical creatures have appeared in traditional Japanese myths, stories and art. Today, they are the heroes and villains of Japan's manga comics and anime. These "spirited beasts" from Japan's past have become pop culture superstars, known and loved around the world.

A Spirited Beast Becomes a Modern Superstar

Truly unique, Epcot® Theme Park's message is best captured in its nightly firework display "IllumiNations: Reflections of Earth." Widely considered one of the most spectacular nighttime shows ever produced, IllumiNations takes viewers on a journey around the globe as music and pyrotechnics tell a story of hope and promise for our world.

With each country offering several restaurants, and eleven countries to choose from, Epcot® boasts an endless smorgasbord of enticing options. *Disney elements ©Disney Enterprises, Inc.*

Walt Disney hoped that those leaving EPCOT would take pride in humanity's ability to change the world for the better. Above all, he hoped that this new sense of pride would inspire them to build a brighter tomorrow in their own communities. Even though his true vision was never realized, it's clear that his ideals were universal—and are still very much alive in Epcot® today.

Hopefully, a visit to Epcot® will stay with guests long after they exit the park gates. *Disney elements ©Disney Enterprises, Inc.*

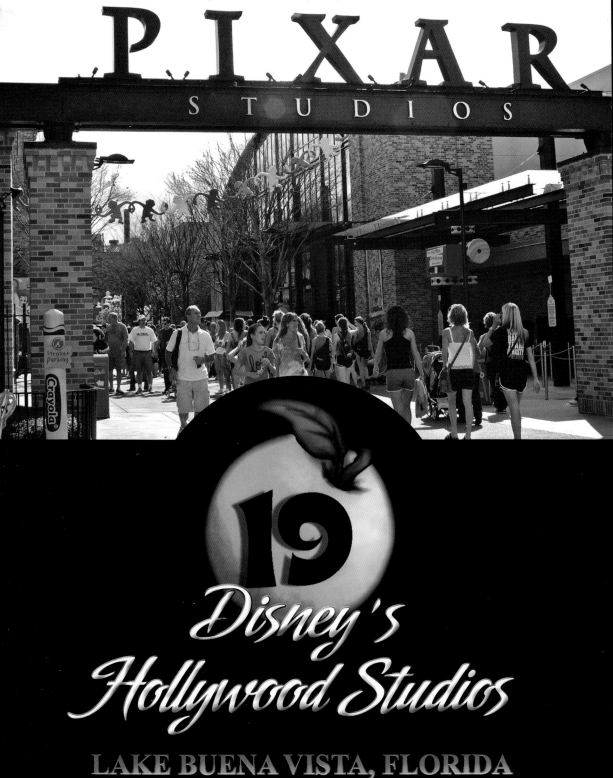

Known for films like *Finding Nemo*, *Monsters, Inc.*, and *Up*, guests can now tour a section of the park themed after the beloved animation studio, Pixar. *Disney/Pixar elements ©Disney Enterprises, Inc./Pixar.*

PIXAR STUDIOS

19

Disney's Hollywood Studios

LAKE BUENA VISTA, FLORIDA

Mickey's sorcerer hat can appropriately be found center stage in a park dedicated to movie magic. *Disney elements ©Disney Enterprises, Inc.*

Originally intended as the anchor attraction of Epcot® Theme Park's movie pavilion, plans for The Great Movie Ride quickly expanded—creating an entire new park in the process. *Disney elements ©Disney Enterprises, Inc.*

DEDICATED TO HOLLYWOOD—NOT A PLACE ON A MAP—but a state of mind that exists whenever people dream, wonder, and imagine, Disney's 3rd Walt Disney World® Resort theme park opened on May 1st, 1989. Originally intended as a movie pavilion in Epcot®, Disney CEO and Hollywood Studio veteran, Michael Eisner, suggested transforming the plans into a new theme park embracing entertainment and show business. Unlike Disney's other theme parks, Disney's Hollywood Studios® isn't broken into lands, but features several themed areas, laid out much like a working studio.

Offering apparel with appeal, Mickey's of Hollywood and other stores like it line Hollywood Boulevard to satisfy all guests' shopping needs. Those who know their Disney trivia may recognize that this store shares its name with Mickey's of Glendale, the gift shop at Walt Disney Imagineering's main California campus. *Disney elements* ©Disney Enterprise, Inc.

MICKEY'S

OF HOLLYWOOD

APPAREL

Part of the park's vast show ensemble, Lights, Motors, Action!® Extreme Stunt Show® offers a window into how car chases and vehicle action sequences are shot and translated to the big screen. *Disney elements ©Disney Enterprises, Inc.*

Hollywood Boulevard, which functions as the park's "Main Street," is lined with fabulous boutiques and souvenir shops—like the real street of the same name. At the far end of the walk, guests are invited aboard The Great Movie Ride, a twenty-two-minute tour through classic film scenes and great Hollywood moments.

In a park dedicated to Hollywood movie magic, visitors can expect an abundance of great shows. In Echo Lake, one of the park's larger themed areas, guests will enjoy Indiana Jones™ Epic Stunt Spectacular!, an exciting spectacle with scenes reenacted from the popular film franchise. Then, board a star speeder on the newly re-imagined Star Tours®, or take the stage and compete with other guests at The American Idol Experience.

On a thirty-five-minute tram and walking-tour, guests will learn the ins and outs of what goes into a major studio production. *Disney elements ©Disney Enterprises, Inc.*

Get an up-close look at how water, fire, and earthquake effects combine for an explosive result in the Catastrophe Canyon portion of the Studio Backlot Tour. *Disney elements ©Disney Enterprises, Inc.*

For those interested in learning about what goes on behind the scenes, the Studio Backlot Tour is a must. Visit costume and prop departments, and see how editing and special effects are used to create blockbuster films. Afterward, stroll through the rest of the park's themed area, Streets of America, and notice how the facades change from California to New York in just one block.

Like a real city, the Streets of America continue off into the distance...or do they? Sometimes it can be difficult to make the distinction between illusion and reality in this Hollywood-themed park. *Disney elements ©Disney Enterprises, Inc./Pixar.*

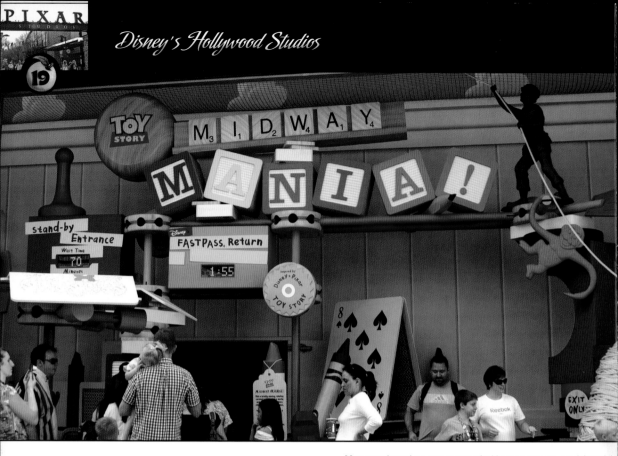

TOY STORY M₃ I₁ D₂ W₄ A₁ Y₄ MANIA!

Mosey on through an assortment of midway games on a rootin' tootin' ride the whole family will enjoy. The 4D style of play will have guests lobbing virtual baseballs, pies, and darts at moving Toy Story-inspired targets. *Toy Story Mania!® attraction is inspired by the Disney®Pixar's Toy Story films. Disney/Pixar elements ©Disney Enterprises, Inc./Pixar.*

Animation enthusiasts will enjoy the park's newest section, Pixar Place, which is modeled after the renowned computer animation studio in Emeryville, California. Take aim for the highest score on Toy Story Mania!®, one of Disney's most innovative theme park attractions. Then, learn how Disney animators bring characters to life in the park's Animation Courtyard. Animation fans may also be interested to learn that the park formerly operated as one of Disney's satellite animation studios and was the birthplace of several animated films like *Mulan* and *Lilo & Stitch*. Finally, discover the man behind it all at Walt Disney: One Man's Dream.

Next stop—thrills! Aptly named, Sunset Boulevard features some great attractions best experienced at twilight. *Disney elements ©Disney Enterprises, Inc.*

Travel in style on this high-energy coaster as your super stretch limo careens through La-La Land and off to the red carpet. *Disney elements ©Disney Enterprises, Inc.*

CHECK RADIO FOR
TRAFFIC INFO.

Take a memento home for everyone. You don't have to be a celebrity to deserve an award. *Disney elements ©Disney Enterprises, Inc.*

Music groupies and adrenaline junkies will likely find Sunset Boulevard the most exciting spot in the park. Buckle up for a limousine ride like no other as you race through L.A. to a concert on Rock 'n' Roller Coaster® Starring Aerosmith. Drop in to The Twilight Zone Tower of Terror™ for a thirteen-story free-fall on a haunted elevator, or enjoy a performance of Fantasmic!, the park's iconic "Nighttime Spectacular."

With all the glitz and glamour of America's "Tinsel Town," Disney's Hollywood Studios® will wow those who love big screen entertainment, and want a close-up look at how film magic is created.

20

Disney's Animal Kingdom

LAKE BUENA VISTA, FLORIDA

Of course, Disney's Animal Kingdom® offers more than just land animals. With several aquariums and even a stage show inspired by everyone's favorite lost clownfish, guests can be assured that our aquatic friends are also well represented in the park. *Disney elements ©Disney Enterprises, Inc.*

With multiple aviaries, guests will encounter a wide variety of exotic birds strolling the walkways alongside guests. *Disney elements ©Disney Enterprises, Inc.*

INSPIRED BY WALT DISNEY'S PASSION FOR ADVENTURE, Disney's Animal Kingdom® opened on April 22nd, 1998, and is dedicated to all animals—real, ancient, and imagined. Driven by a commitment to conservation, the park features a variety of walking and safari tours over more than 500 acres, making it the world's largest Disney theme park. Out of respect for its animal inhabitants, the park tends to close earlier than others at the Walt Disney World® Resort, and unlike most Disney Parks, it does not offer a nighttime fireworks show.

As guests traverse the park's seven themed lands, they will notice one thing that unites them all: lots and lots of *green*. Through the entry Oasis and onto Discovery Island®, sharp-eyed guests will enjoy spotting anteaters, boar, and many more animals who call the lush foliage their home. With over 250 species, the park's total animal count is well into the thousands. At the center of the park, the 145 foot tall Tree of Life offers a fantastic accolade to the world's many creatures, with over 300 animals carved into the bark.

The perfect playground for paleontologists-in-training, The Boneyard® features an archeological dig site, musical fossil bones, and plenty of secrets just waiting to be unearthed! *Disney elements ©Disney Enterprises, Inc.*

Chester and Hester's Dino-Rama, a colorful area within DinoLand U.S.A.®, features a handful of midway games and rides, including the Primeval Whirl® spinning coaster. *Disney elements ©Disney Enterprises, Inc.*

From Discovery Island®, guests can then choose between the park's other themed lands. At Camp Minnie-Mickey, the Greeting Trails provide a chance to meet up with a few vacationing "characters," while Festival of the Lion King presents a high-energy tribal celebration. DinoLand U.S.A.®, offers the chance to pick up a shovel and uncover dinosaur fossils; or the opportunity to head back in time on the exciting DINOSAUR, to save the last great lizard from extinction.

Many of the park's attractions are in lands far from civilization. Africa features the Kilimanjaro Safaris® Expedition, where open air vehicles take guests through the vast African savanna, where animals roam freely together. Those preferring to trek on foot are invited to explore the Pangani Forest Exploration Trail®. From Africa, guests can also board a train to the remote Rafiki's Planet Watch®, a land dedicated to conservation and co-habitation—complete with a petting yard.

Heading east, guests arrive in the exotic land of Asia. With a similar walking tour, the Maharajah Jungle Trek®, guests can discover animals native to the region, including tigers and giant bats. Sometimes the best way to explore uncharted lands is by raft, and those seeking to escape the midday sun will enjoy the exhilarating whitewater trip down the Kali River Rapids®. Finally, a trip to Asia would not be complete without a mountaineering expedition to the Himalayas. Scale the world's tallest Disney peak, at Expedition Everest®—but beware of the mythical creature that guards the sacred ground. Strange things happen to those who don't heed the warnings!

Guests onboard the Kilimanjaro Safaris® Expedition get an up-close look at African wildlife. *Disney elements ©Disney Enterprises, Inc.*

Groups may encounter other families as they tour the savanna. The wide open spaces allow the animals to move freely—as they would in the wild. *Disney elements ©Disney Enterprises, Inc.*

At Rafiki's Planet Watch®, discover how we can better share our world—and our own backyards—with animals. *Disney elements ©Disney Enterprises, Inc.*

Spending a total of six years in development and construction, Expedition Everest® was the world's first $100,000,000 roller coaster. The final results included a new skyline for the park, a twenty-two-foot tall Yeti, and one of the most exciting rides ever built with a roller coaster train that travels forwards … and backwards! *Disney elements* ©*Disney Enterprises, Inc.*

ANGOLAN

For centuries, inhabitants of Nepal and Tibet have warned outsiders of a legendary Himalayan guardian. Those who choose to proceed would best be advised to do so with caution. *Disney elements ©Disney Enterprises, Inc.*

The park offers a unique opportunity to literally come face to face with many other species. Occasionally, it may just be difficult to tell who is studying who. *Disney elements ©Disney Enterprises, Inc.*

LACK & WHITE COLOBUS MONKEY

A.M. OBSERVATIONS

- Woke to loud calls by the colobus males. They were probably announcing their feeding area to other colobus groups.

- Monkeys spent most of the morning feeding on tree leaves, buds, and shoots

P.M. OBSERVATIONS

- Individuals in group were observed grooming each other

- Highest ranking monkey received the most grooming

I continue to see fewer and fewer animals. This overhunting for bushmeat has caused serious declines in colobus and populations across Africa.

Aaron M.

Disney's Animal Kingdom® presents a chance to not only observe animals, but to learn more about them as well. Specialized cast members are always on hand to answer questions. *Disney elements* ©*Disney Enterprises, Inc.*

The ideas of conservation have deep roots within The Walt Disney Company. Walt Disney believed it was important for people to understand and embrace the natural world; his True-Life Adventure documentaries took viewers to remote locations around the globe, allowing them to see the behavior of animals in the wild. Today, visitors can explore the natural world and experience some of those exotic locations, all within the lush, green space of Disney's Animal Kingdom®.

TIMELINE

1878: A New Window to the World: Hullam Jones invents the glass bottom boat at Silver Springs.

1971: A Theme Park Pinnacle: Disney opens what would become the #1 family vacation destination and most visited theme park in the world—Magic Kingdom—at The Walt Disney World Resort.

1936: First-Time Flora and Films: Cypress Gardens flourishes in its first year. Silver Springs receives its first major film credit.

1943: An Inadvertent Extravaganza: With just a week to prepare, Cypress Gardens hosts its first waterskiing show.

1949: A Golden Age: The Florida Attractions Association is founded, pioneered by Silver Springs, Cypress Gardens, and several others, ushering in a golden age for Florida's roadside attractions.

1958: New Ideas Begin to Brew: Three years after Disneyland opens, Walt Disney begins contemplating something new.

1973: __If You Build It... They Will Come__: SeaWorld opens its first Orlando theme park as several theme park giants begin following Disney from California to Florida.

1965: __"The Florida Project"__: Walt Disney holds a press conference with Florida governor, Haydon Burns, to announce a major Disney attraction planned for central Florida.

1975: __Expanding the Magic__: Disney opens Downtown Disney, its first dining and shopping area outside a park berm, setting the stage for a much larger resort soon to follow.

1965: __A Zoo Breakthrough__: Busch Gardens expands to include the Serengeti Plain animal habitat.

1963: __A Seaside Success__: Miracle Strip Amusement Park opens along with its classic Starliner Roller Coaster.

TIMELINE

1990: A Major Wrap Party... and a Sequel!: Universal Studios opens its first Florida park after eight years in development and begins planning a second just a year later.

AND HERE!

1989: Disney Expansion... Take Two!: Disney opens its new movie theme park and Typhoon Lagoon, the world's most visited water park.

BUILD HERE!

UNIVERSAL

Water-Skiing!

1982: History, Heritage, and Hallowed New Ground:
-Disney finally opens EPCOT, almost 25 years after the earliest concepts are drafted on the project.
-Dick Pope, owner and founder of Cypress Gardens is inducted into the water skiing hall of fame as "The greatest promoter that the sport of waterskiing has ever known."
-Universal begins drafting its first concepts for an Orlando movie-themed attraction.

1976: A Coaster Revolution: Busch Gardens opens its first roller coaster, the Python, and begins its transformation to the thrilling theme park we know today.

1977: Off to a Splashing Start!: Wet 'n' Wild Orlando opens as the world's first modern water park.

1998: <u>An Unsurpassable Safari:</u> Disney's Animal Kingdom opens as the largest single Disney theme park in the world.

1999: <u>From Parks to Resorts:</u> Islands of Adventure and Citywalk open, transforming Universal Studios Florida into the multifaceted resort we know today. SeaWorld would follow one year later with the opening of Discovery Cove, turning Orlando into its first multi-park destination.

2006: <u>A New Peak in Price Tags:</u> Expedition Everest opens at Disney's Animal Kingdom as the first roller coaster with a nine-digit price tag.

$100,000,000

2010 and Beyond: <u>New Beginnings:</u>
-Miracle Strip enjoys its first season at Pier Park, giving Florida seaside parks a 2nd lease on life.
-Universal's Islands of Adventure opens its first new island, The Wizarding World of Harry Potter, to rave reviews.
-In 2011, Legoland Florida opens on the former site of the historic Cypress Gardens, with a land paying tribute to the former park's rich legacy.